Hugo Reid

Sketches in North America

With Some Account of Congress and of the Slavery Question

Hugo Reid

Sketches in North America
With Some Account of Congress and of the Slavery Question

ISBN/EAN: 9783337009762

Printed in Europe, USA, Canada, Australia, Japan

Cover: Foto ©ninafisch / pixelio.de

More available books at **www.hansebooks.com**

SKETCHES IN NORTH AMERICA.

SKETCHES

IN

NORTH AMERICA;

WITH SOME ACCOUNT OF

CONGRESS

AND OF

THE SLAVERY QUESTION.

BY H. REID.

LONDON:
LONGMAN, GREEN, LONGMAN, & ROBERTS.
MDCCCLXI.

LONDON:
T. HARRILD, PRINTER, SHOE LANE,
FLEET STREET.

PREFACE.

This little volume has its origin in a belief that, at the present time, when the condition of the American Republic is creating such intense interest, some account of the Slavery Question, which has led to the great events going on there, and of the Parliament of the Union, might be welcome to English readers. To these I have added a few sketches of various points of interest that have come under my notice in North America.

Our American friends need not be surprised that British writers should mark particularly those points in which we may suppose that their institutions are not working satisfactorily. We have a tendency in the same direction; and it is very important for us to gather any indications we can of where that direction leads. There are spots on the sun; and there is so much genius, greatness, and goodness in the people of the United States, that they can well afford to admit a few defects mingling with these. Desirous of avoiding exaggeration or misrepresentation of any kind, I have, by extracts from papers and speeches, as much as possible, made the Americans describe themselves.

The extraordinary development of energy, liberty, and intellectual life, in the United States of America, at once strike the traveller as something great—something new, that is seen in no other nation on the face of the globe. This, and the friendly feeling everywhere evinced towards the British visitor, make travelling through the States very agreeable indeed, and rub off not a few prejudices. Doubts and difficulties may occur to him, but an impartial observer cannot avoid seeing in the people of the United States a truly great nation, exciting in the highest degree his interest, admiration, and warmest wishes for their welfare.

LONDON, *March*, 1861.

CONTENTS.

CHAPTER I.
YANKEE 9   PAGE

CHAPTER II.
CONGRESS 76

CHAPTER III.
THE SLAVERY QUESTION 155

CHAPTER IV.
AMERICAN CITIES—HOTELS—SCHOOLS—WOMAN IN AMERICA 222

CHAPTER V.
NOVA SCOTIA 276

SKETCHES IN NORTH AMERICA.

CHAPTER I.

YANKEE.

"Would he were fatter!"—*Shakspeare.*

"Jonathan may be described as the finished model of the Anglo-Saxon, of which John Bull is the rough cast."—*American Magazine.*

AFTER a long sojourn in that dullest of all dull places, Halifax, Nova Scotia, I was at last released for a time, and set out to have a peep at Brother Jonathan. Nova Scotia is almost an island, the neck of the peninsula which connects it with the mainland being only sixteen miles in breadth, and it is difficult getting out of Halifax to any place worth going to. The nearest place of any interest is Boston, in the United States, and the most direct way of escape thither from Halifax is by steamer or sailing-packet, a voyage of nearly two days in the British mail-steamers, the best vessels that run between the two places. There is another route to Boston, by railway to Windsor, on the Bay of Fundy, across the bay by steamer to the city of St. John, New Brunswick, and thence by a coasting steamer to Boston, or to Portland, in Maine, from which there is railway communication to Boston; the whole journey being accomplished in about three days, of which a night is spent at St. John.

When so much money has been spent on railways in British America, the traveller is disappointed to find that there is no railway route from Halifax to the United States, nor even to Canada. Railways in Nova Scotia have been adapted, not so much to the wants of the country as to the purpose of securing influence and votes for a political party. There is little traffic in the country, little prospect of any material increase, and a small population of about three hundred thousand, thinly scattered over a country more than half as large as Scotland; while every part being so near the sea, the coasting-trade will always retain a large share of the transport business. Passenger traffic with the great nations near them, and the railway connection of Halifax (the port on the continent nearest Europe), with Canada and the United States, were the only chances for railways to be of use in the lower British provinces. Instead, however, of pushing their railway system to connect Europe with America, and to connect themselves with the Canadian and American railways, and thereby with a restless, active, trading population of more than thirty millions, the most travelling people in the world, the Nova Scotians and New Brunswickers have looked chiefly to their slight internal trade, in planning their railways. The consequences are that last year in Nova Scotia the total proceeds from the railway were about £2000 short of the working expenses, and the Government is now making a desperate effort, by sweeping reductions of the salaries of subordinates, to preserve for their railway the decent appearance of paying at least the cost of working it; in New Brunswick one principal railway was not working at all, being at a dead stand, the chief sign of life about it being the mansion of the manager, who had little or nothing to manage, at the terminus, the largest and most stylish-looking house in the village; while the traveller who desires to pass between Halifax and Canada, or the United States, must be subjected to a tedious and dangerous voyage, and the Canadian visiting Europe, during six months of the year, must pass through a foreign country, and embark and disembark at a foreign port—Portland, in the United States. It appears surprising that lines of communication so obviously wanted as from Halifax to Canada and the United States, have not been accomplished yet. The colonies seem to have exhausted themselves on lines of but secondary importance, fifty years in advance of trade and population, and to be waiting for assistance from England. One cannot avoid wondering that countries so lightly taxed, and with such a thriving population, should look for aid to the British, who are so heavily taxed, and are oppressed by so fearful an amount of pauperism. But the colonies are ever crying for " more."

In the middle of April, 1859, I set out from Halifax by railway for Windsor, on the Bay of Fundy coast, a distance of about forty-five miles. The railway is a single line, constructed for the Government, and, like many railways in America, exhibits marks of haste and scanty means. The banks are steep, and the curves many and sharp; and, as if sharp bends are not of themselves sufficiently objectionable, one of these is placed where the line crosses a deep lake, or, rather, arm of the sea, so that if by any accident the train runs off the line at the sudden turn it is plunged into deep water, and the passengers are sure to be drowned if they escape being knocked to pieces. One feels a little nervous at this dangerous pass, and as I had to go through it rather frequently, I may perhaps be excused for having a lively recollection of it.

Another alarming looking railway drive is that between Philadelphia and Baltimore, where the line crosses some inlets of Chesapeake Bay. It is laid upon piles, which scarcely rise above the water, and the train seems to be skimming over the surface without any solid bottom to support it. The engineers may be satisfied, but to the uninitiated it looks very unstable and somewhat alarming.—For about twenty miles from Halifax the country is rocky and barren, everywhere the ground is covered with huge stones, masses of granite, or of the metamorphic sandstone, which extends along the whole Atlantic coast of Nova Scotia. Although it was the middle of April the lakes were still frozen, there were yet no symptoms of reviving vegetation, and what with the stones thickly strewed over the soil, the stumps of trees in some places, in others tall bare trunks, remains of forest conflagrations, and the chilly aspect of the frozen lakes, I have seldom witnessed such a scene of desolation. With frosts and heavy snows from November to March, and a cold ungenial spring in April and May, one cannot but sympathize with the brave and hardy pioneers of civilization settled in this wilderness. Towards the Bay of Fundy coast there is much alluvial deposit and disintegrated trap; the soil is rich and fertile, and this side of the peninsula is usually described as the garden of Nova Scotia. The north side, also, adjoining the Gulf of St. Lawrence, is more productive and enriched by mines of good coal near Pictou. In the north-east of the province, at Sydney, in Cape Breton Isle, there is a very fine coal, which, as well as that from Pictou, is largely exported to Halifax and other places in British America, and to the United States.

Windsor is a small village, situated on the estuary of the Avon; a narrow channel, up which we may see the famous Bay of Fundy tide rushing with a furious rapidity that appears very striking to one accustomed to the gentle rise of the tide on most of the British coasts, and in remarkable contrast with the tide at Halifax, on the opposite side of the peninsula, which rises and falls only from five to seven feet, its movements being almost imperceptible. At Windsor, the rise of the tide is about forty feet; but it reaches upwards of sixty feet in some places on the Bay of Fundy. There are large quarries of gypsum, or plaster, as it is usually called, at Windsor; from which about 57,000 tons, valued at £11,200 are exported yearly to the United States, partly for manure, partly for stucco. The other exports from this little village are potatoes, some hides, cattle and sheep, and considerable quantities of the fish called shad, and halibut, also sent chiefly to the United States.

In America we are often agreeably surprised at meeting familiar sounds, reminding us of home, in the names of rivers, counties, towns, etc., as Windsor, the Avon, the Trent, the Mersey, the Thames, the Clyde—tokens of the early settlers' cherished recollections of their native land. But the traveller is more pleased still when he meets the names given to the rivers, hills, etc., by the aborigines, which are often retained; those strange combinations of sounds that bespeak, as surely as face or form, another race that possessed the land before the intruding Caucasian. In Nova Scotia and New Brunswick, the land of the Mic-mac and Millicete Indians, we find many picturesque native names still preserved, with *sh* of very frequent occurrence, as Mush-a-mush, Shubenacadie, Missaguash, Musquodoboit, Musquash, Digdeguash, Magagaudewek, Washademoak, Oromocto, Chebucto, Chignecto. There is yet a third class of names found in these provinces, which cannot be said to be picturesque or romantic, or to have any pleasing or striking association mingling with their sounds as they strike the ear; such are Salmon River (there is no end of Salmon Rivers), Folly River, Great Village River, Half-way River, Nine-mile River, Inhabitants River, West, Middle, East Rivers, and so on. The names of the counties of Canada present a singular medley of historic associations : Huron, Ottawa, Kamouraska, Missisquoi, Arthabaska, tell of the Red Indian, the original lord of the soil; Champlain, Beauharnois, Richelieu, Montmorency, Montcalm, recall the chivalrous nation that first colonized, from Europe, the banks of the St. Lawrence; Wolfe, Wellington, Peel, Lambton, Elgin, Russell, remind us of the sturdy Anglo-Saxons who overthrew the first colonizers of Canada, and now rule this great country. The towns of Lower Canada are full of odd admixtures of names. In Montreal we find such incongruous sounds as *Rue* McGill, *Rue* Wellington; and among the signs above the stores in a leading street in that city may be seen the classic French name of *Cinq Mars*, side by side with the homely Scotch name James Boyd, Grocer.

Such is the strange jumble of names we meet with in many parts of America; there is a similar jumble of people, feelings, ideas, which it will require centuries to dissolve, or to fuse —I am afraid the process will be a fiery one— into a homogeneous mass.

At Windsor it was pleasing to meet with a little oasis in the surrounding intellectual desert —King's College, a real college, with able and accomplished men for its professors. Shut up in this remote little village, cut off from the society and intellectual life of Europe or the United States, which they would at once enjoy and adorn, these gentlemen have still a noble task before them. They are sowing the seeds of a higher intelligence, of superior tastes and refinement, in this young province, where the effect of their labours will be felt in time, though these are hardly yet appreciated as they should be. Colleges, D.D.'s, and LL.D.'s are easily, cheaply, and quickly got up in North America, where, in fact, they spring up like mushrooms. Many of the so-called colleges are little better than schools, and as to the D.D.'s and LL.D.'s, the less that is said about them the better. I have seen in respectable American papers serious remonstrances as to the reprehensible facility with which such honours may be procured. But King's College, Windsor, is of a higher class. While open to all sects, it is under the direction of the Protestant bishop, and the leading Episcopalians in the province. Though not a large body (about 40,000), the Episcopalians in Nova Scotia, as in the United States, are the *élite* of the land; and in this small province it is to them that it is due that anything like a collegiate education or instruction in the sciences can be had. But for them there would be no chair of the French and German languages, no professor of chemistry or geology in the country. The college is maintained chiefly by the liberal contributions of the Episcopalian gentry, aided by a small grant from the Government. The province is under great obligations to the supporters of the college at Windsor, who, by their liberality and unwearied efforts, amid many discouragements, thus provide for the youth of Nova Scotia the means of procuring a first-class education. Other sects have institutions for training up their youth to the ministry. Were the different sects to unite and have one college in the capital, a noble institution might be maintained there, the only place where there could be a prospect of any considerable number of students. They could have the chairs of secular knowledge, as classics, mathematics, chemistry, in common, while each sect might have its separate theological department. Such a scheme, however, implies a certain amount of common sense and Christian charity and good feeling between the different religious bodies. A population of three hundred thousand cannot maintain more than one efficient college; but there is so much sectarian bitterness and animosity in this little province, that there is no prospect of such a union for many years to come. At Windsor College I feasted my eyes with the view of a library with many learned-looking quartos and folios, of retorts and crucibles, various philosophical instruments, and other scientific and educational *matériel*, the like of which had not blessed my sight for some years.

I left Windsor in the morning, by steamer, for St. John. There had been a fall of snow during the night, and the ground was covered to the depth of several inches. We reached St. John after a pleasant passage of about nine hours, not being delayed by hazy weather, rather an uncommon event in the great region of fish and fog. I hardly any other time arrived at a port in these provinces without being detained by fog. The next time I went to St. John, the passage was about twenty-four hours, during twelve or thirteen of which we were tossing about off St. John, till we got information from some fishermen as to our whereabouts. St. John has a very fine natural harbour, with a considerable amount of shipping in it, and seems an active stirring place. The houses are of wood and brick, with some fine stone buildings. The town is at the mouth of the noble river of the same name, the sail up which to Fredericton, the capital of the province, is one of the finest I have seen.

We left St. John at eight in the morning, in a Yankee steamer, with the engine-beam playing above the deck, and other peculiarities of construction that distinguish American steamers. One of these seems deserving of imitation; the steersman is in an elevated position near the bow of the vessel, so that he has the best view that can be had of whatever may be in the ship's course. About noon, we reached Eastport, where we stayed a short time. This is a small town or village, situated on an island at the N.E. of the State of Maine, and, like most of the American towns I saw, strikes one immediately by its clean, neat, cheerful aspect. In fact, it is quite a charming little village; most of the houses are of wood, nicely painted or whitewashed, and almost all tastefully constructed; they are generally detached from the adjoining houses, and each has a small garden around it, prettily laid out. There are trees in several of the streets, as in many towns in America; and, extending beyond the suburbs, I found a luxury to which I had not lately been accustomed—side-walks of planks, so that in the worst weather, one can get a clean, pleasant footing in every part of the village. Eastport is in the State which, by the boundary treaty of 1842, so inconveniently indents the British provinces, and which has become famous as the inventor of the prohibitory liquor law. This enactment is so far successful that a stranger passing through Maine unprovided with private pocket companions, and unacquainted with the ways of the place, is compelled to be very temperate. I found, however, on a subsequent visit, that good things are to be had easily by those who know the where and the how, and that the Maine Liquor Law is chiefly effective as an obstacle to a traveller getting a refreshing glass of ale or porter, but little impediment to the people of the town procuring what they may require. The House of Assembly of Nova Scotia passed a prohibitory liquor law lately, for which several members voted, quite against their convictions, to please their constituents, but in the hope that the Upper House (the legislative council) would throw out the bill; which that body did, much to the gratification of the Government, the real majority of the Lower House, and the intelligent part of the community. As the revenue depends almost entirely on import duties, Nova Scotia, by the extraordinary facilities it affords for smuggling by its extensive sea-board, is the last country in the world where such a law could be enforced.

At Eastport, I had the first sample of the fire and energy which characterize the Yankees. A variety of goods had to be put on shore, and I stood on deck watching the operation, which was the most rapid go-a-head scene of the sort I ever witnessed. The men did not walk quietly and soberly up the gangway with the heavy packages or wheelbarrows; they leaped, jumped, ran, now a porter with a great box on his shoulders, now a seaman, driving a wheelbarrow before him, now some one pushing up a barrel, all rushing up with their burdens and flying down for a fresh load, as if they were running for their lives, and chasing one another with a sort of mad fury, like so many comical devils in a pantomime. It was my first view of Yankee going-a-head, and, slight as the incident was, impressed me strongly with a sense of the fire and intense activity of the people.

At about four in the morning the vessel arrived at Portland, the chief port in Maine, at the S.E. of that State, and there I left the steamer, to proceed to Boston by railway, a journey of about five hours.

The American railway carriages gave me the first specimen I had of American "equality," and in their comforts and superior accommodation for all classes, showed that the "sovereign people" were a real power in the United States, and had to be attended to. There is only one class, and that class has a comfortable seat with cushions to sit upon and cushions to lean back on, in closed, but cheerful and well lighted carriages, that are properly warmed in cold weather. The people are cared for there; we do not see in the United States anything like the miserable third (and some second) class carriages found in this country, not only uncomfortable, but by the cruel exposure, injurious to the health, and that must, in this cold and wet climate, have proved fatal to many aged and delicate persons. An American is thunderstruck when he sees the carriages in which *the people* have to travel in this country, thanks his stars he is not a citizen of a State where the masses are systematically subjected to such discomfort and degradation, and wonders at our anxiety about the slaves in America, and our neglect of the slaves at home, for such he considers the winter occupants of third-class carriages on British railways.

The American railway carriage (or *car*, as it is called) though not so luxurious as our first-class carriage, has some important advantages even over it in construction. The entrances are by doors at the ends, up safe, easy, wide steps, very different from our precipitous, dangerous ascents and descents at the sides. The car is open from end to end, not divided into compartments. A passage is kept between the two doors from one end to the other, and the guard (or passengers) can walk with perfect ease and safety through the carriages, from one end of the train to the other, instead of scrambling outside, at the risk of his life, as we often see the guard doing in trains on this side of the Atlantic. The passengers can rise, walk to the doors, and get the benefit now and then of a change of posture and a little motion; while persons selling newspapers, magazines, books, or refreshments for the body, are frequently passing through the carriages. The seats, each holding two persons, are placed across the car, on each side of the passage, the passengers facing the end of the car; and, by an ingenious, but very simple mechanism, the backs of the seats are moveable, can be turned to either side of the seat, so that the passenger can sit facing either way, as he may prefer. A party of four can thus sit, two facing two. In winter, two of the seats are removed, and a stove is put up with standing-room around it, and any one can go from his seat to the stove, warm himself thoroughly and return. In the European railway carriage, one feels quite cramped, "cabined, cribbed, confined," after enjoying the ease and comforts of the American car. From the number of people in view, their movements, the privilege of rising, changing one's seat, going to the door, from the entrance of persons with newspapers, etc., for sale, the time passes much more quickly and pleasantly in an American car than in the European one, in which one soon feels oppressed by ennui and weariness of soul. It is also deserving of notice that in the American trains, the passengers, guards, and drivers have easy communication with one another through the cars, which can be traversed quickly from end to end.

The defects of the American cars, as compared only with our first-class carriages—for

they are immeasurably superior to the others—
are, that the back of the seat is not high enough,
there being no support for the head and neck,
no soft, snug corner to nestle in, while the seat
is rather short for two—at least for two goodly
Britishers; perhaps it may do for two lean
Yankees. On a railway on the broad guage,
between, I think, Elmira and Canandaigua, in
the west of New York State, the latter defect
does not exist, and there I saw the most comfortable cars for a short journey that I ever met.
On long journeys, for half a dollar, one can get
a bed made up in a sleeping car, where, if we
do not sleep, we at least get rested, and in the
recumbent posture—a very important point in a
night journey of ten or twelve hours. On the
great lines for passenger traffic, as between
Boston and New York, the case of the lovers of
tobacco is considered, and "smoking cars" are
provided.

It would be an improvement in the American
car were there some comfortable seats with high
backs, as in our first-class carriages, where also
one might be a little quiet (we must not say
" select," in the United States), and not in the
midst of a restless crowd. But I suspect that
such exclusiveness would not be tolerated in the
great republic; it would be considered " aristo-

cratic." In matters of public accommodation, all must be served alike. The " sovereign people " are fully impregnated with the doctrine which Jefferson laid forth in the Declaration of Independence, that all men are created equal, and they have " bettered his instruction," to make it mean somewhat more than he ever intended by it.

There are excellent arrangements also as to the baggage. It is given in charge to a baggage-master, who gives in return something to show for it—a brass ticket with the number marked in bold characters. When the train is approaching a leading station, an agent of one of the *expresses* (for forwarding goods) comes into the cars, and, if you are willing, on receiving your check, will take charge of your luggage, and forward it to any hotel or other address you give him; and you have no trouble hunting up your goods; you can go immediately to your abode, where they will soon follow, if they are not there before you. Attached to every engine there is a large, loud-tongued bell, which is always rung when a train starts, and when it is approaching a station where it is to stop—a useful signal to passengers waiting the arrival of a train, and which may also be a preventive of accidents.

While speaking of railways, I may mention that, in several instances, I found great want of punctuality as to the arrival of trains. In some long journeys, where I had a through ticket, for a succession of railways under different companies, one train was often too late for the connecting train; and I was sometimes detained hours, a day, or two days (if Sunday intervened). This occurred repeatedly to myself, and I knew of many other persons experiencing the same irregularity; not from unexpected accidents, or impediments caused by the weather, but from sheer negligence and indifference to keeping faith with passengers. It seemed as if the companies were in league with the inn-keepers on the line, who were the only parties benefited by the failure to perform what the advertisements held out, what could easily be done, and what the ticket was sold for. I found the Hudson River Railroad Company particularly distinguished for such want of good faith; the delays on that line were frequent and shameful, such as I do not believe ever occur on any European railway, and quite discreditable to any public company. Another unpleasant thing on the American railways was the disagreeableness of the conductors, the only class of people in the United States, that came under my notice, of whose manners I had cause to complain. Cold, disobliging, and repulsive, one could with great difficulty extract any information from them, and yet a stranger is greatly dependent on them; as the companies do not provide satisfactory time-bills, with the clear, full, exact information one finds in Europe. Comparisons are odious, but I could not help contrasting the behaviour of the American conductors with the frank, hearty, obliging manners I have ever found in like officers on the British or Continental railways.

The Americans exhibit extraordinary fertility of invention. When railways are established, and a large carriage is required for the new mode of conveyance, we stick together three coaches of the old sort, and even paint the new one so as to look like the old one. The American takes advantage of the necessary enlargement to improve the construction, and strike out something new. The Englishman has a large inventive genius, but at the same time a tendency to stand by the old ways; the American assumes at once that whatever is old is wrong, and never rests till he has hit upon something new. This spirit of innovation greatly promotes invention. Ingenious and convenient contrivances for saving time, trouble, and expense, as well as promoting comfort, abound everywhere in the United States. This inventive spirit is encouraged by the easy terms on which patents may be secured. The following is the tariff of fees for patents and caveats, which, with one or two of the regulations, show that everything is done to foster and promote improvements in the useful arts.

	DOLLARS.
Application for a design	15
Caveat	20
Application for a patent, if made by a citizen, or a foreigner who has resided in the States for one year, and made oath of his intention to become a citizen	30
Application for a patent—	
By a subject of Great Britain	500
By any other foreigner	300
Application for an extension	40
Copy of a patent or other instrument, 10 cents for every 100 words.	
Recording the assignment, 1 dollar up to 300 words; 2 dollars for 300 to 1000 words; 3 dollars above 1000 words.	

On a patent following a caveat, the charge for the latter is allowed to stand as part of the fee for the patent. An extension, after inquiry and hearing of objections, is granted for seven years.

If the application for a patent is rejected, two-thirds of the charge are returned. It is refused if "the same has been invented or discovered by any other person in this country prior to the alleged invention or discovery thereof by the applicant, or has been patented or described in any printed publication in this or any foreign country, or has been in public use or on sale, with the applicant's consent or allowance, prior to the application." If the description is defective and insufficient, the Commissioner of Patents "shall notify the applicant thereof, giving him briefly such information and references as may be useful in judging of the propriety of renewing his application, or of altering his specification, to embrace only that part of the invention or discovery which is new." There is a Commissioner of Patents, with a salary of 3000 dollars per annum, with an efficient staff, consisting of clerks, a draughtsman, and a machinist, and several principal examiners, with a salary each of 2500 dollars, and assistant examiners, with a salary of 1500 dollars per annum. Each of these has charge of some particular class of inventions. The patentee must "furnish a model of his invention, in all cases which admit of a representation by model, of a convenient size, to exhibit advantageously its several parts." This is deposited in the Patent Office.

The PATENT OFFICE at Washington is one of the sights of the country. This is a huge building, with four sides and a court within, not much less than Somerset House. It is constructed mostly of white marble, in the Doric style; and in it are deposited specimens of the subject of every patent taken out. The collection, as may be supposed, is overwhelming. The nation is teeming with ingenuity, and ever producing something new; everybody invents or improves something, takes out a patent, and deposits his model or sample in the Patent Office. I believe the people of the United States surpass every nation on the globe in the number of new inventions yearly produced. If this inventive spirit continues, and the population goes on increasing as hitherto, ere long all Washington will hardly suffice for a patent office. Last year no less than 5638 patents were applied for, and 846 caveats were registered. Three thousand eight hundred and ninety-six patents were issued, and twenty-eight extended for seven years from the expiration of the first term. The income of the office for last year was 197,648 dollars (about £40,000 sterling), and the expenditure 189,672 dollars, showing a surplus of 7976 dollars. In the Patent Office a variety of antiquities, curiosities, and other objects of interest, are deposited—as the press at which Franklin worked in London; the coat worn by General Jackson at the battle of New Orleans; the coat worn by Washington when he resigned his commission at Annapolis; various treaties, as with Louis XVI.; the Declaration of Independence (a second copy, with the real signatures; the original, or first copy, is preserved in the State-Paper Office).

Grates and stoves have yielded great scope for American ingenuity; the variety of these is extraordinary. The cooking-stove is now beginning to be used in this country, and perhaps we might find it worth while to adopt some form of the grate very generally used in North America. I do not know that it is originally an American invention, but the practical people of the United States have appreciated its advantages. In places where fuel is dear, its use would be greatly conducive to comfort and economy. It is an open grate, giving a sight of the fire and the cheerful blaze so welcome to the Englishman; but it is not, like our grate, imbedded in the wall, sending half its heat up the chimney, or into the dead mass behind it. It stands out from the wall a little, throws out heat on all sides into the room, not only by radiation, but by direct contact with the air of the room, which touches it on every side; and really gives out the whole heat produced, excepting that small portion which must ascend the flue in the warm column of air that creates the draught. It need not project further into the room than the present fender, gives no offensive odour, and, in the newest forms, is fitted with doors and regulators, and every desirable convenience. In a place like London, where the cold is sometimes severe and fuel very high in price, one of these American grates would, I feel confident, be a boon in many a family. In the Northern States anthracite, a non-bituminous coal, that burns without flame, like coke, is much used, often in stoves, instead of grates. These stoves are sometimes ill-constructed, and give out a most deleterious gas, the frequent inhalation of which must be very injurious to the health.

The first thing that interested me, on arriving in the United States, was the *look of the people*—a point on which I had considerable curiosity, so much has been said *pro* and *con* as to an alleged change in the form and features of the Anglo-Saxon race after a settlement of some generations in America. About seventy years since, in a work published in 1788, Dr.

Smith, President of Princeton College, asserted that then a change had begun to take place in the inhabitants of European descent, in both complexion and feature, consisting in an approximation to the Indian type. Dr. Knox holds that the climate of America causes the Anglo-Saxon to degenerate, and that already the United States' man differs materially from the European. Dr. Pritchard was informed that the heads of Europeans in the West Indies approach those of the aboriginal Indians in form, independently of intermixture. Dr. Carpenter thinks that, in form of cranium and cast of countenance, the Anglo-American races are growing like the North American Indian; and the same doctrine is upheld by a recent writer in the "Protestant Episcopal Magazine," of New York.* These opinions have been violently

---

* Dr. Morton, the distinguished American ethnologist, regarded this notion as "wholly idle and gratuitous." But he himself held "the doctrine of *primeval diversities* among men—an original adaptation of the several races to those varied circumstances of climate and locality which, while congenial to the one, are destructive to the other." Assuming this adaptation of race to soil, etc., it does not seem unreasonable to suppose that "circumstances of climate and locality" may, in time, cause an intrusive race to assimilate in some degree to the race for which the region was specially adapted. This doctrine of the original diversity of races is

protested against by American writers, and at present no very positive proof can be adduced on either side. It is difficult for one who is but a short time in the country to distinguish between the native descendants of old settlers and descendants of recent immigrants; and when we find that since the close of the last war with the United States no less than three millions of persons have emigrated to that country from the United Kingdom alone, it is evident that care is necessary in forming an opinion on the subject.

Still one cannot avoid acquiring some impression, and the conviction on my mind is that the Anglo-Saxon has changed considerably in America; that he is there lean and spare in

gaining ground in the United States. Its leading supporter is AGASSIZ; and two large works, by Messrs. Nott and Gliddon, have been published, mainly intended to enforce and illustrate this theory—"Types of Mankind" and "Indigenous Races of the Earth." Agassiz says: "The boundaries within which the different natural combinations of animals are known to be circumscribed on the surface of the earth coincide with the natural range of distinct types of man." At the same time, Nott and Gliddon maintain that geographical influences, even in a long series of years, can effect no material change in a race. This part of the theory is a favourite with the pro-slavery party, who infer from it that the negroes never can improve so as to be fit for freedom.

form, slim, agile, with sharp features and an anxious expression; the females thin, pale, and delicate-looking. Brother Jonathan is sadly changed (improved, he says) from that grand, portly-looking John Bull, whose look and figure are so familiar to every one who has travelled in England. Seldom in the United States do we meet the rosy lass or stout burly fellow so common in the old country. Very few are enormously fat and unwieldy-looking. One does not meet there (or very rarely—probably a born Britisher) the large, rosy, well-rounded, full-paunched John Bull, without a wrinkle in his chubby cheeks, or a sign of care in his whole countenance—the personification of ease, content, good humour, and much beef and beer, so well described in the lines—

"Round as a globe, and liquor'd every chink,
Goodly and great, he sails behind his drink."

These lines find no illustrations among our western cousins.

The Americans themselves admit that they have, in point of fulness of outline, deviated from the British type. One American writer says, "Contrast the lean, lank, lackadaisical Yankee with the ruddy, round, and robust

Englishman, his ancestor." Another remarks, "The Americans are, undoubtedly, a thin people"—" they may, probably, have a worn look" —"they have too much to do, and are too anxious to do it well, to allow of the necessary repose for the quiet accumulation of fat."—" Our women have not the *embonpoint* of the English, but they don't imbibe London stout by the imperial measure, nor retire to their couches torpid with strong-brewed ale and old Stilton." While amused by the explanations, we may accept the writer's admission of the facts. He says also that Jonathan, compared with John Bull, " is more cleanly cut, his proportions more regular, his features more sharply chiselled and his action more free."*

On no occasion did this difference strike me more forcibly than on entering the British Mail Steamer at Boston, suddenly encountering the

* The rest is too good to be lost: "The latter is altogether too superfluous and clumsy; his proportions want regulating; his belly is too protuberant; his neck too thick; his feet too spreading; his hands too large and podgy ; his lips too spongy and everted ; his cheeks too pendulous ; his nose too lobular, blunt, and bottle-like ; his expression altogether too beef-eating. In a word, according to our taste, John Bull won't do, and must be done over again."—" The American is an Englishman without his caution, his reserve, his fixed habits, his cant, and his stolidity."

British physiognomy, with the American one quite fresh in my recollection. It was like coming amongst a different race. The seamen, stewards, waiters, seemed so sleek, fat and rosy, altogether so easy-going, content and comfortable-looking, it was difficult to imagine that they had the same origin as the lean, hard, wiry, quick, restless, anxious-looking American. That both men and women of the Anglo-Saxon race undergo a great physical change in the United States, I think there can be little reason to doubt. Whether that physical modification is to be termed degenerating, or improving, as some Americans think, time will show. Mentally, there seems no decrease of vigour.

But the Americans cannot be spoken of now as one race; climate and institutions are developing at least two sections, nearly as distinct as British and French, or English and Irish— the North and the South.

While all are more spare in figure than their cousins in the old country, the Southerners seem, in other respects, to have deviated least from the type of their ancestors, having the quiet and composed bearing of the English, with much resemblance to them in look and manner; and with the advantage of, I think, less of the coldness and reserve which too much characterize the latter. We know that, when roused, they are impatient and fiery, reckless of life and vindictive, ever ready, for a mere trifle, with the bowie-knife or the revolver; still, the gentlemen of the Southern States appear to me more like the English in look and bearing than any other class of persons I saw in the United States, and very different from the generality of the inhabitants of the North.

But the Northerner, the New Englander, the real Yankee—in him we see a new race springing up. Spare in face and figure, he is distinguished by a clear penetrating eye, a singularly intellectual aspect, a frank, open expression, a quick, impulsive, nervous manner; his bearing is marked by restlessness and a sort of explosive energy; there is no repose in his character; one feels quite slow beside a genuine New Englander. His temperament seems in a high degree nervous-sanguine, with the former element preponderating. He has a constant craving for action, for change, for excitement. He is the very embodiment of the spirit of scheming, speculation, and enterprise, has faith in himself, goes-a-head with a reckless confidence and headlong stick-at-nothingism, and, more perhaps than any nation on earth, exemplifies the Scotch saying, "He will make a spoon or spoil a horn." He often does spoil the horn; but, with wonderful elasticity, springs up again, perhaps on the very spot where he fell, like a Phœnix from the ashes—perhaps in the far west, into which he carries the same dash and daring. An American and Nova Scotian were discoursing of banking, after the crisis of 1857. The latter was praising the banking system pursued in his province, in which, he said, the banks never fail. "What, sir," said the lively Yankee, "your banks never fail!—*the people can have no enterprise.*" That remark is a perfect picture of the disposition of the New Englander. He is a great character; he has made New England the envy and admiration of all America; and has filled the great west with his genius and his institutions.

Dispersed everywhere through the United States, another countenance is to be seen, resembling neither the Englishman, the Southerner, nor the New Englander. In many Americans, one finds a peculiar and well-marked expression, like the grave, grim look of the North American Indian. This, denoted by a long compressed upper lip, a marked expression of firmness, with little adaptation for a smile, I had noticed in Americans whom I had seen

D

in England, many years ago; and found not a few examples of it in travelling through the States, though not so many as I had anticipated. Is this the Puritan or the Red Indian type? And if the latter, is it the result of an ethnographic modification produced by the climate, or is it to be traced to Indian blood in the veins? Possibly it may be, as the writers above referred to have supposed, that the climate and soil—the geographical influences of America— have a tendency to develop the Indian type; and that this appears only in those of the Anglo-Saxons who, by constitution and character, are already predisposed towards it. It does not seem likely that this change of expression will go far or extend to more than a few; but that it has taken place to a certain extent, there seems every reason to believe, whatever explanation may be found for it.

In another point the look of "the people" struck me forcibly, compared with the appearance of the lower classes in Europe. While all are somewhat spare or lean, few are very lean; the great body of the working classes in the British Colonies, as well as in the United States, look well fed and comfortable; very few, indeed, are to be seen there, like the "needy, hollow-eyed, sharp looking wretch" so frequently met with in the large towns, and amongst the peasantry, too, in Europe. Pinching poverty seems rare; all seem to have enough. It is distressing, on returning to England, to see the vast number of poor—very, very poor—that abound everywhere. In four weeks, in the vicinity of London, I have seen more wretchedness, and been accosted oftener by beggars, than in four years in North America. Nova Scotia, New Brunswick, and other parts of the British Settlements are crying out for labour. It seems hard that we can neither bring the food to these poor people, nor send them to it. Such is the present advantageous position of the lower orders in America; but it is alleged that there are already visible indications of an unfavourable change. Grim poverty is beginning to show itself in the crowded regions of the Atlantic coast, as the outlets in the far West are becoming closed up. The pauperism of the State of New York is said to exceed, in proportion to the population, that of England and Wales. I have not access to reliable statistics on the subject; but in an article in an American paper of standing, it is stated that in this great State, while in 1831 there was 1 pauper to 123 persons, the proportion has been gradually increasing, till now 1 out of every $13\frac{1}{2}$ is a pauper. This might, in some degree, be anticipated as to New York, the State in which the great majority of poor emigrants disembark; but the amount of poverty is understood to be excessive, even allowing for that. And the evil is not showing itself there only.

In the United States, it is delightful to see the bright, animated, intelligent look of the working man, and the air of dignity and self-respect that distinguishes him. We see in these, in the superior tone of address that characterizes him, and in his whole aspect and bearing, the results of early education, comfortable circumstances, taste and opportunities for intellectual pursuits, of the universally diffused feeling of "equality," and perhaps also of the political privileges he enjoys. To the American "common people" much more than to the British, are Goldsmith's lines applicable :—

"Stern o'er each bosom Reason holds her state,
With daring aims irregularly great;
Pride in their port, defiance in their eye,
I see the lords of human kind pass by;
Intent on high designs, a thoughtful band,
By forms unfashioned, fresh from Nature's hand;
Fierce in their native hardiness of soul,
True to imagin'd right, above control;
While e'en the peasant boasts these rights to scan,
And learns to venerate himself as man."

But there is another side to the picture. In England, the upper classes and the employers are apt to be proud, haughty, and disdainful towards the classes beneath them. In the United States it is the reverse ; the employed and lower classes are those who have a tendency to be saucy and insolent; their feeling of independence runs to excess in that direction, the result of comfortable circumstances and of the feeling of equality, and the general jealousy of the upper classes. One seldom meets in an American store, the polite, attentive, almost obsequious manner and anxiety to oblige that characterize shopkeepers in England. An American calls that "cringing," and scorns it— sometimes carries his way a little too far, and so scorns to be civil. Such persons in the United States are often quite regardless and indifferent; don't seem to care much whether you are attended to or not, and won't put themselves in the least about to serve you (I should say, *traffic* with you—*serve* is not the word for America). Frequently on entering a store, not a soul has moved to see what I required, and it was at times a matter of some difficulty to find from several careless attendants which was the right one to apply to. I speak here only of those who owe some duty or service to another, and are at the same time of the less educated and polished classes; such persons are very often so independent and morbidly afraid of exhibiting any obsequiousness, that they run into surliness or sauciness. Along with this, there is a most unmistakeable air of self-confidence in all classes, including females and the young. The air of perfect self-possession, seen in the young, the women, and the lower classes, is surprising; quite different from anything I have seen elsewhere.

From my short experience of the Americans, I should say too much has been written about such small matters as the nasal twang, inquisitiveness, and spitting; and too little of the frank and agreeable manners of the people and their friendly behaviour to strangers. The nasal twang is comparatively rare, though sometimes very well marked, especially in Boston, where I have heard it amongst the legislative officials. It is scarcely heard in Congress. Having travelled thousands of miles in the States, I seldom experienced that inquisitiveness so much talked of, and can only recollect of one occasion on which spitting was in the least annoying. We do meet in the States people a little brusque and eccentric in manners, but not more in proportion than in other countries, allowing for the American hotel and railway systems, that bring all classes together, for the independent character of the people, that prompts a more free and outspoken bearing, and for the comparative isolation in which, in so large and newly settled a country, many must reside. Take the great majority of the people in any considerable American city, they will be found as courteous and well bred as in other cities, and, perhaps, more affable and accessible than the like classes in Great Britain. Now and then one does meet with an unpleasant combination of cold English reserve and surly American independence. But this is rare and exceptional. That peculiar repelling look which characterizes many in England, as if they were indignant at something, and would be greatly astonished if you should presume to address them, is seldom seen in the United States, where, in general, the people are frank, hearty, and open, ready, when travelling, to converse pleasantly, and so aid in passing the time agreeably. Always excepting at dinner in a hotel; there, I must say, I did not find Brother Jonathan inclined to be sociable; he would answer politely, but not encouragingly, in such a way as to convey the impression that he was engaged in a very important business, requiring his undivided attention, for which his time was rather limited, and so did not care to be interrupted. The silence at the dinner-table in many of the American hotels felt sometimes oppressive; at other times, ludicrous, when one looked around, and saw a hundred or two deeply intent and quite absorbed in the great work of cramming, opening their mouths only for the admission of victuals, or to call for more, and heard nothing but the footsteps of the waiters, the subdued tones of the various orders, and the clatter of plates and dishes.

Fluency of language is undoubtedly a characteristic of the Americans. They are trained to it early; they have an extraordinary number of school-books on elocution, and are frequently called on in their schools to speak out, give demonstrations, and recite. They are constantly reading, listening to, or making speeches, and certainly appear to me to have a much readier command of words than the British. You never hear an American hesitate, no hum-and-hawing, failure in finding a word, going back to reconstruct the sentence: their fluency, propriety, and readiness of speech are surprising. I heard a great variety of speakers in Congress; all spoke with perfect freedom and fluency, quite at ease and unembarrassed, with a facility that evinced not only considerable previous practice, but a great natural command of language. The majority were new members, of whom, however, it is probable that many had been members of some of the State legislatures. *Diffidence* is scarcely to be met with in the United States, which greatly promotes fluency of speech. Had Shakspeare lived in modern America, he would hardly have written—

> "Where I have come, great clerks have purposed
> To greet me with premeditated welcomes;
> Where I have seen them shiver and look pale,
> Make periods in the midst of sentences,
> Throttle their practis'd accent in their fears,
> And in conclusion, dumbly have broke off."

"Periods in the midst of sentences" and "dumbly breaking off" are unknown in the United States. Glib and voluble, but at the same time correct and forcible in language, Brother Jonathan is ever ready with words; and, I should suppose, never finds himself in the awkward "fix" in which we sometimes see a rash John Bull, bashful, blundering, and stammering, who has mistaken his vocation, and imagined he had a mission to make a speech. The "gift of the gab" is a national characteristic — according to some of themselves, a national nuisance. A gentleman was applied to for a contribution to assist in establishing a debating society in his native village. He wrote back that he would gladly subscribe *to stop it*, if he could; that there was too much talk already; that he was quite sick of it; that the gift of the gab would be the ruin of the country. It is even denounced from the pulpit. In a fast-day sermon a clergyman said, " The people of this country have talked too much, have written too much. Verboseness is one of the national sins." But they do talk well, and by talking train the mind as well as the faculty of speech, and are better able to exhibit their talents and information.

One cause why the Americans deviate from the British type may, I think, be adduced to explain some points in their character and physical constitution. They are not the descendants of the *average* of the British, but of certain sections only. The stout, corpulent, jolly-looking John Bull does not leave his country; he is at ease, and content, and does not need to emigrate, which would be too much trouble to him. He stays at home, and enjoys " mine ease in mine inn." The Americans are, for the most part, the descendants of the disappointed, restless, uneasy, lean, and discontented part of the English—

"All the unsettled humours of the land."

A constant succession of immigrants of this peculiar description must, in time, give rise to a different national character. This, with the Puritanical descent of many, may explain several of the characteristics of the American features and character. At the same time, the large amount of the Celtic element among the settlers must also produce its share of the change, and aid in forming the lively, restless Yankee, in place of the more sober, staid John Bull. When his heterogeneous elements become thoroughly intermixed he will be a compound mainly of English, Irish, and German, and, if the influence of climate and institutions permit, will probably be an improvement on the original stock.

Climate must also have some effect in the transformation going on. Though we do not as yet know much as to the action of air, sun, and soil, we can hardly doubt that a change from the damp, cloudy, temperate clime of Great Britain to the great summer heat, severe winter cold, comparatively dry atmosphere and serene sky and sunshine of North America must affect the physical constitution considerably, and probably also have some action on the mental characteristics.

Education and institutions also contribute their share. From their very childhood the Americans are inured to driving and excitement. The rousing and animated style witnessed in the infant schools is continued and maintained during youth up to manhood, when declamation, fiery debates, and never-ending political struggles, keep up the eternal turmoil. All are educated, all have votes and political influence, and all are in a state of continual excitement on public questions. Every four years the country is stirred to its foundations on the presidential election, the agitation for which is in full operation a twelvemonth beforehand. Every two years a new Congress is chosen; and besides this each State has its own legislature and governor to elect at short intervals. Every city has its little parliament, and the citizens of each State must attend, more or less, to the doings of the other States. Last year there were three long messages requiring the particular attention of the inhabitants of the city of New York—the President's message, the State Governor's, and the Mayor's.

New territories are being settled, for each of which laws and a constitution are wanted; the settlers are turned into as many Solons, and on the principle of go-a-head, or "Excelsior," they strive to produce something more perfect than ever was known in the world before. The tendency is ever onwards, going further and further in the direction in which they began; liberty, equality, restriction of the authority of judges and rulers, and the principle of government by the governed are pushed to an extreme. Great public meetings, conventions, caucuses,* platforms, demonstrations, are for ever going on. In short, every man is a sovereign, perpetually occupied in governing the other sovereigns. Thus the nation is kept in a continual ferment. We may question if so cumbrous a system of government, and so much legislational turmoil, are for the good of the country; but who can doubt that they must produce an excitcable, quick-witted, restless people. Thought and the power of speech are developed,

---

* A *caucus* meeting is a select preliminary meeting held to prepare a course of action at the legislative assemblies, some important convention, or other public meeting. A *platform* is a declaration of the principles of a party—that upon which they stand; each leading point is a *plank* in the platform, and we sometimes hear even of a *splinter* of a plank.

with self-confidence and presumption, for all are equal, and all are powers in the state. Public life is fostered, home discouraged, and a morbid craving for excitement created.

There can be little doubt that from all these causes a new national character, a new race-variety, widely different from the British, will grow up in the United States. The Americans seem approximating to the French in character: in exciteability, impulsiveness, restlessness, and fluency of language, they are already far more French than English. It is quite a pleasure to see the intelligence and animation which characterize all classes. They are indeed a remarkably clever people, and we must hope that there will remain amongst them enough of the solidity (or stolidity, as the Americans call it) of the Anglo-Saxon to preserve this truly great nation from the dangers to which they are exposed by their cleverness and impulsiveness, and the trying circumstances and institutions with which they have to contend.

No man can have lived a little in North America, whether in the United States or the British Colonies, without perceiving that impatience of restraint and a morbid jealousy of rulers penetrate the whole system of society. The lower classes, servants, the employed, the young, the women, in short, all who have any one above them in authority or standing, are in a state of chronic insubordination. There is no organ of veneration in North America; every one in authority is looked upon with suspicion; as a possible oppressor, who must be narrowly watched, and checked at the slightest manifestation of his natural tendency to be a tyrant. This is seen in the audacious bearing of the young, in the rowdyism in even the old-settled large cities, not always confined to the mob, in the intolerance of the federal authority by the several States, and of the State authority by its citizens, and in the increasing tendency to give the people the election of judges, and to appoint them for limited times only, thus placing the judgment-seat in subservience to king mob. The "Boston Courier" states, "The philosopher of Concord informed his fellow citizens that it was on general principles 'the duty of the States to resist the United States Government, of the cities to resist the States, and of the villages to resist the cities.' Why the philosopher stopped there, we do not know. He ought to have added that it was the duty of each household to resist the municipal authority of the village, and of each individual to resist the head of the family." The "Courier" might have added that there really is, in the American mind, an impatience of control and constant tendency to resist, that renders government very difficult indeed. It appears as if America had but two cardinal points in her political creed, derived from the Declaration of Independence, that all men are equal, and therefore no one should be subject to the control of another, and that all in authority tend to be tyrants, and thence the people have the right to resist their governors; and as if it was felt to be a duty, as well as a right, to take every possible opportunity of calling into action these fundamental principles of trans-atlantic government.

The case of "the philosopher of Concord," referred to by the "Courier," well illustrates this spirit of resistance. This was a Mr. Sanborn, a teacher of that place, who, backed by other philosophers and the House of Representatives, at Boston, had the honour and glory of bidding defiance to the Senate of the United States. A committee of that body had been appointed to inquire and report as to the John Brown insurrection at Harper's Ferry, with power to send for persons and papers. The committee proceeded to summon as witnesses various parties, who, it appeared, had been in communication with Brown, with the view of throwing some light on the subject. Of the persons summoned, or expecting to be summoned, some found it convenient to disappear, others gave evidence under protest. Mr. Sanborn was bolder; he would neither testify nor run away. Having paid no attention to the summons, the sergeant-at-arms was instructed to bring him before the House, and an officer was sent by the sergeant to arrest him. The officer went to Mr. Sanborn's house in the evening with a carriage and several assistants, and Mr. Sanborn refusing to go with them peaceably, they were dragging him by force to the vehicle, when his cries brought down his sister; she called out "murder" most lustily, alarmed the neighbours, and it is said, got the whip and lashed the horses, so that the marshal's men were occupied in holding them, and he could not force Sanborn into the carriage alone. Soon the crowd who had gathered protected him, till some one ran to a judge's and got a writ of *habeas corpus*, which a deputy-sheriff served, and took the prisoner from the hands of the marshal. On this writ, Sanborn was brought before the Supreme Judicial Court of Massachusetts, at Boston, and liberated on the ground that the sergeant-at-arms must execute the warrant himself, and cannot, unless

E

specially authorized, depute to another the duty of arresting a recusant witness. It was understood that there were innumerable other pleas for resistance in reserve. This might be good law, but it is remarkable that the Senate proceeded no further in the matter; that the House of Representatives at Boston took it up and evinced a determination to support Sanborn, even while the question was in the hands of the judges; that at a public meeting at Concord, resolutions were passed, justifying Sanborn's resistance, declaring that " resistance to tyrants is obedience to God," and organizing a Vigilance Committee to protect him for the future; while it is also said that determined and well-armed men attended the court, and had carriages ready outside, to rescue him and carry him off, should the decision have been adverse to him.

It was with great regret that I observed many evidences of this turbulent and disloyal spirit in Massachusetts. That little republic is the gem of America; one sees there so much to praise, so much to excite admiration and respect, so complete and highly-finished a piece of workmanship in state-craft, that one is sorry to find its perfection marred by any serious defect. A book might be filled with descriptions of the excellent institutions for government, police, reformation of juvenile offenders, education, literary and scientific research, collection of statistics, and the general advancement of all classes; betokening a humane and highly enlightened spirit pervading the whole body of the people. In the Legislature and Law Courts, in its celebrated Harvard University, and its admirable system of public schools, in its literary, scientific, and historical societies, its public libraries and lectures, its periodical press, and the more enduring literature it produces,* its men of science, historians, statesmen, its enterprising merchants, bankers, manufacturers, its neat, clean, cheerful-looking towns, its well-cultivated fields, and trim gardens, the numerous common roads, railroads, docks and harbours, and other public works, one sees innumerable signs of not only an energetic and a thriving population, but of a fine-spirited, well-ordered, intellectual community. And all this—which

* The Newspaper Press of Boston is of a very superior character indeed; and from that fine city emanate the two foremost periodicals of the United States—the "North American Review," and the "Atlantic Monthly;" and one of the best Almanacs in the world—the "American Almanac;" while the "Massachusetts Annual Registration Report" is one of the most complete things of the kind produced in any country of the world.

will compare favourably with any of the oldest and most highly-civilized States in the world—all this has been created out of the wilderness in little more than two hundred years! Massachusetts is truly a model republic; admirable in itself, its influence for good has spread over the whole of that vast country, to which it sets a thousand excellent examples; if it could add one more, that of respect for the law and the government, it would be almost perfect.

Nothing is more striking to an Englishman, accustomed to the respect for, and instant submission to, the law, which prevail in Britain, than the turbulent disregard of the legal authorities and their decisions evinced in the British Colonies and the United States. A remarkable instance occurred in Nova Scotia lately.

A leading member of the government was convicted of bribery by the Election Committee that tried the case. This was a terrible blow to the government; they had but a doubtful majority of only two or three, and one vote lost might be ruin. Besides, this was by far the most respectable man of the party; his character and standing were of even more consequence to them than his vote. It was determined to support him at all hazards. It did not matter that the decision of the Election Committee was that of the court established by law for trying such cases; that its members were sworn, heard evidence and counsel, had the witnesses confronted with them, and cross-examined in their presence, and sifted the case carefully and anxiously for weeks. The decision was reversed immediately by a hasty party vote of the House of Assembly, without any form of trial at all, without hearing or even having an opportunity of reading the evidence. It was a desperate position; the party had just grasped the reins of office after waiting for three years; was the cup to be dashed from their lips? No! a little *coup d'etat* would save their man and their places; and so legal forms and the established constitutional modes of procedure were set at defiance, and it was carried by a majority of two or three that black was white and might was right. The same party, a short time before, had, in their anxiety to gain a vote, given notice in the House of Assembly, of a motion to expel a member who was not even petitioned against, and put one of their own friends, who had contested the election in his, place. They shrunk, however, from going on with this outrageous project; some said, because they found they could secure their majority without it, and thought it prudent not to be so very wicked without an urgent necessity; while others alleged that they had a hint from a very high authority that this was "rather too bad."

It is sometimes supposed that the British Colonies differ much from the United States, because their governments are formed upon the British model. But although the form is there, the spirit is wanting; the institutions are British, but the working of them is altogether American. The influence of the Imperial Government is little felt; the wide extension of the suffrage and the want of a class of high-minded independent men for statesmen (or the shrinking of that class from public life), produce the same fruits as in the United States—a feeling in the mob that they are the supreme authority, a disrespect for the law, a turbulent spirit of resistance against rulers, and the elevation of an inferior class to stations of honour and influence.

The jealousy of rulers and judges, and the increasing tendency to limit their authority as much as possible, and reserve power in the hands of the people, are remarkably evinced in the laws of the new States, or recent regulations of some of the older States, as to the appointment of judges. *These appointments are being trans-*

ferred to the hands of the people, and conferred for a limited time only. In Massachusetts the judges are chosen by the Governor and Council for life, or during good behaviour. In North Carolina, South Carolina, and Rhode Island, they are elected by both Houses of the Legislature, during good behaviour. But in most of the other States they are elected by the people, and for limited terms only—from 15 years in Pennsylvania, to 8 (in New York), 7, 6, 5, and 4 years, the latter being the rule in Arkansas, California, Georgia for the county judges, Indiana (by a new law in 1859), and Virginia. In New Jersey the judges are appointed by the Governor and the Senate for 6 years; in Connecticut (since 1855), by the two Houses of the Legislature, for 8 years; in Vermont they are elected annually by the Legislature. A Massachusetts paper, referring to the interference of the Legislature in the Sanborn case, alluded to above, expresses its apprehensions that the constitution of that State, following the general tendency, may be so altered as to place the election of the judges in the hands of the people and so make the judiciary a mere instrument for registering the decrees of the majority for the time being; and a New York paper states, "the system of electing judges is rapidly raising the rogues of this city to the dignity of a third estate." With judges who are the nominees of the people for short periods only, and juries who are, as De Tocqueville says, "the judicial committees of the majority," one cannot wonder that the law commands little respect in the United States.

Rowdyism is a characteristic feature of North America, by no means confined to the United States, though there it is certainly most rampant. It extends also to the British Colonies, and even sits enthroned in high places there. A new term is found readily in America when it is required, and assuredly the word "Rowdy" was much wanted. It seems to mean a rough, violent, disorderly, unscrupulous person, with no respect for law of any sort, determined on having his own will, by whatsoever means, and ready, in the lower forms, to lie, cheat, bully, strike, stab, or murder, in order to get it. Rowdyism seems an institution peculiar to the new world. In Europe, there is no lack of violence or murder, prompted by revenge or the hope of plunder; these, too, occur abundantly in America, but in addition there are numerous deeds of violence or assassinations, following a hasty word between persons utterly unknown to each other, and there is a large class predisposed to such actions, ready, like the Malay, to "run-a-muck." Rowdyism cannot be ascribed alone to the present weakness of the governments. I am afraid we must trace it further back; like that other giant evil of the United States, slavery, it is an inheritance from colonial times. The early colonists were in the condition most favourable for the development of rowdyism. Many were very rough, lawless sorts of persons; they had a wild, uncultivated country around them, and had to go armed, to defend themselves from Indians and savage animals; they had a ready escape to the backwoods or the prairie from the arm of the law; and instead of a strong government, which the circumstances of the case required, the colonial authorities inspired neither awe nor respect, had no adequate means of maintaining the supremacy of the law, and were despised by the people as the mere feeble delegates of a power at the safe distance of thousands of miles of ocean. Even had British institutions been completely carried out, and strong local governments been implanted in America, with a body of men to administer them who commanded respect, the peculiar condition of the country must have led to some amount of this evil; but with such a proportion of rough, desperate men amongst early settlers, rulers who did not inspire respect, and Governments without force to back them, the wonder is that the evil is not even more developed than it is.

Rowdyism, which thus originated in the circumstances of the early settlers, and the deplorable weakness of their rulers, has doubtless been fostered by the institutions of the republic, and the emigration of great numbers of ignorant, violent, disorderly persons since the last war, and is now rampant in some of the oldest cities in the Union, as Baltimore and New York, where, if anywhere, one should have expected law and order to be firmly established. The extent to which the spirit of murderous rowdyism prevails in the large cities, is frightful and almost incredible. In the city of New York, not long ago, rowdyism and assassination had reached such a pitch that the authorities felt themselves called upon to enforce the extreme penalty of the law upon a youth little more than seventeen years of age, who had wantonly killed a man by stabbing in a street riot. In Cincinnati, last summer, a professor in a college there, returning home at night with two ladies, heard some offensive remark from a knot of rowdies loitering at a corner; he imprudently turned back towards them; in a few seconds the ladies heard a cry, and on looking for their friend, found him alone, dead on the street, stabbed to the heart with a bowie knife. There is no reason to believe there was any private revenge to gratify; it is supposed that his reproof or remonstrance led to angry words, followed by the fatal blow with the ever ready bowie knife. Baltimore, in 1859, exhibited an extraordinary series of crimes. A man was convicted of arson; his brother assassinated the policeman who was the chief witness against the incendiary. The brother was tried for this murder and convicted; thereupon, a comrade, repeating the very crime for which the brother was tried, avenged him by assassinating another policeman who had given evidence against his friend. For these and other murders, four men were executed at Baltimore shortly before I visited that city, and the landlord of the hotel at which I lived, told me, with an air of confidence, that they had now put down rowdyism, and that the city was peaceable and safe. This sense of security, however, was but short lived; at the ensuing municipal elections dreadful riots took place, at which fire-arms were used, many were wounded, and four or five citizens were killed. Nor is this turbulent spirit confined to the lower classes; the better classes are ever ready to take the law in their own hands and accomplish their ends by deeds of violence when legal means fail. The recent destruction of the buildings at the Quarantine Station, Staten Island, was the work of a higher class of rowdies—and no one has been punished for the outrage.

This fearful rowdyism—this turbulent spirit of resistance to authority—is the great evil of North America—worse than slavery; for the latter is local and must, ere long, come to an end; the other is universal, no one sees how it is to be checked, and we cannot but look forward with great anxiety to the time, slowly, but surely approaching, when population will press upon the means of subsistence, when the far west will no longer afford an outlet, and the eastern regions will be crowded with a dense mass of needy and desperate persons. That I have not given an exaggerated view of the extraordinary development of this turbulent spirit, will I think be evident from the following statements, extracted from respectable New York papers, which the reader will find well worthy of his attention.

"An extraordinary state of things is prevailing here [Baltimore]. The law, the press, nay, public opinion itself, is boldly defied by organized gangs of ruffians, who pillage our citizens by day and assassinate them under cover of the night. The credit of our city has been sadly tarnished within the last two or three years by the bloody tumults which have broken out in our streets, and which our authorities, through fear or supineness, have failed to check or punish.

"We have in Baltimore some three clubs, or fraternities of reckless and abandoned men, known under the grotesque appellations of 'Plug Uglies,' 'Rip Raps,' and 'Black Snakes.' These men have no bond of union but the lowest dissipation, and no motive to confederation but riot and bloodshed. At all our elections these last three years these gangs of cut-throats have driven from the polls, with clubs and pistols, all classes of our citizens, until the franchise has become a nullity. But their violence has not stopped here.

"Our energetic District Attorney, Mr. Milton Whitney, who prosecuted the assassin Gambrill on Friday, is in hourly danger of his life. Attempts were made to shoot him as he left the court-house. Captain James, warden of the city jail, had to call in the aid of forty policemen, armed with muskets, to protect the prisoner, Henry Gambrill, from the desperate attempts to rescue him after his conviction on Friday last, by the ringleaders of the clubs and their followers. These unparalleled outrages would never have been heard of but for the impunity which has attended previous crimes. Look at our criminal records for the last three months. A chief of the Plug Uglies named Chapman, enters a drinking saloon surrounded by his myrmidons, demands drink, and refuses to pay for it. The unfortunate barkeeper remonstrates, and is shot dead by Chapman, who receives three cheers for this atrocious murder.

"At any hour of the day or night, you may be stopped by a facetious 'Plug Ugly,' who informs you that his club intends giving a ball next week, and he presents forthwith some four or five tickets, price one dollar. If, sensible of the honour, you take the tickets and give up your money, it is well; but should you be ignorant of the consequences, and refuse, you are knocked on the head and rolled into the gutter. I appeal to the citizens of Baltimore if this be not the actual condition of our city."

* * * * *

"The boldest criminals escape in the face of the most clear and irrefragable proofs. What is the matter?

"We will tell you, gentle reader, what the

matter is; and we will tell you that the matter is not, as is generally charged, with the judges or the laws. Never had country better laws than ours; and in the main, at any rate, in the open adjudications of the bench, the judges are upright and correct; but the true trouble is, that *the People are corrupt!* The maxim of 'All's fair in politics'—operating upon a population relaxed by an overwhelming prosperity, cursed with a preternatural sharpness, and haunted with that love of place which makes murderers and perjurers of kings—has debauched the morality of the whole nation, and prepared every man to look with more or less lenity upon the various phases of corresponding guilt. The 'all's fair in politics,' that will carry a man to the poll to swear in his vote, will instruct him, when he comes away, to defraud his partner; to cause the bookkeeper to make false entries, the clerk to plunder his employer's drawer or forge his name; while nothing is easier, for one and all of them, than to violate or to forget a juror's oath, in favour of parties whom they have become accustomed to regard as no worse than themselves. In view, therefore, of this rapid deterioration of society, we can see no remedy but in such alteration of the jury system as to cure this thirty-three and one-third per centage of deterioration in the public mind. The jury system was devised in a country where the people were less *fast* than here. It was founded on the theory that the community was pure, and that twelve perfectly honest men could easily be drawn to agree in any case that required a decision. That the basis of this theory is gone, so far as this country is concerned, it needs no argument from us to urge; and, being gone, we consequently find ourselves in the dilemma of an inevitable necessity for change. This change was proposed by us, in other journals, in the shape of two-third verdicts, years ago.

"We fear the continuance of the present state of things. We wish to see a practical remedy applied, before the increasing irritation bursts into fury, and ends in the unmanageable storm of revolution. The taxes this year, in this single city (New York) amount to more than eight (?) millions of dollars; almost every public officer is a plunderer of the treasury; and criminals cannot be convicted, because of the public sympathies with crime. It is a fearful contemplation for a citizen who loves his country. In other lands, when laws are oppressive, and dynasties become corrupt, the indignant people rise in general in revolt, and crush their tyrants into atoms; the vengeance over, they sink again into repose and satisfied submission: but, when the new régime becomes as corrupt and oppressive as the old, they rise once more, and sweep that, also, to the winds. At every tornado the atmosphere is purified; and the masses, which performed the work, being honest in themselves, a term of comparative happiness and good government is secured. Here is an alternative and a remedy; and, consequently, always a ray of hope. With us, all rational hope is gone. So long as the rulers of a people only are dishonest, Liberty is safe; but what is to become of a nation, the people of which are corrupt."

* * * * *

"The 'Boys' of New York. — In New York, on the 'Fourth of July,' a gentleman was quietly standing on his door-step; a troop of young rowdies was passing by, when one of the number thrust his knife into the breast of the unoffending citizen, and left him bleeding to death at his own door. Referring to this dastardly act, the New York *Tablet* says of the 'boys' of the city:—

"'If there be in the world a class in which every moral instinct is dead, which bears, under a human shape, the heart of a hyena, and the combined savage instincts of all the meaner wild beasts, that class is surely the so-called "boys" of New York. Treacherous, cowardly before equal, not to say superior, force, blasphemous, fearing no authority, divine, parental, or legal, immoral and unclean in word and deed, they are the very lowest specimens of humanity, and it is difficult to parallel them among the beasts of the jungle and the forest. The air of our streets is laden with their foul-mouthedness, which daily assails the ears of our mothers, wives, and sisters. Violence to man and woman is their common pastime, and cold-blooded murder their highest enjoyment.'"

* * * * *

"We believe we express only the settled judgment of reflecting men, when we say that *self-government, with universal suffrage, in large cities, has proved a failure.* It does not answer the purpose of government. It does not give us security either for our persons or our property. It does not preserve order or prevent crime. It gives us neither clean streets nor safe walks. It does not check ruffianism nor prevent pauperism. It is neither a terror to evil-doers nor a praise to them that do well. It gives us dishonest law-makers, corrupt judges, and imbecile executives. It elevates

the worst men to the highest places, and stifles
the voices of good men when raised even in
remonstrance. . . This is not the experience of New York alone—every city in America
is showing the same results and teaching the
same lesson."

CHAPTER II.

CONGRESS.

"Most potent, grave, and reverend signiors."

THE legislature of the great American republic is called "Congress," and consists of two bodies—a *House of Representatives*, elected by the people every two years, its numbers being in proportion to the population as ascertained by the decennial census; and a *Senate*, consisting of two members chosen by the legislature of each State for six years. The number of representatives at present is 237; of senators 66. The election of senators was so arranged from the beginning that one-third go out every two years, two-thirds of the body being thus persons of some legislative experience. In the formation of the constitution the smaller States were afraid that their individual interests might be swamped by a legislature chosen simply in proportion to population, and, to conciliate them, an equal voice (two votes) was assigned to each State in the Senate. In estimating the population entitled to members in the House of Representatives, *three-fifths* of the slaves are reckoned along with the free population: the Slave States insisted upon this. Slaves are spoken of in the constitution as "other persons," " persons held to service," "such persons as any of the States now existing shall think proper to admit" (referring to those brought in by the slave-trade). The words " slave," " slavery," do not occur in this famous document, though slavery, and the slave-trade up to 1808, are distinctly recognized and supported by the constitution. The House of Representatives may be said to be chosen by universal suffrage, the rule being, " the electors in each State shall have the qualifications requisite for electors of the most numerous branch of the State Legislature." The Senate represents the individual States ; the House of Representatives, the people as a whole, being based strictly on population. New York elects 33 members ; Pennsylvania, 25 ; Ohio, 21 ; Massachusetts, 11 ; Rhode Island, 2 ; Virginia, 13 ; North Carolina, 8 ; South Carolina, 6 ; Georgia, 8 ; Kentucky, 10 ; Tennessee, 10. The members of Congress have each an allowance of about £600 a-year, besides travelling expenses. No senator or representative can, during the time for which he is elected, hold "any civil office under the authority of the United States." Hence the ministers of state do not appear in either House, and from this arises the very long Presidential message, which is, in fact, part of the ministerial statement for the session. Long detailed reports are at the same time laid before Congress by the Secretaries of the Treasury, of the Interior, at War, and of the Navy, as also by the Postmaster-General. I was informed by some American gentlemen that no material inconvenience was felt from the absence of the leading ministers from Congress; that all requisite information was laid before the Houses by the President; that further information could be had on request by a vote; that adequate checks against misgovernment were provided by committees of inquiry, and by the executive action of the Senate, this body, besides its legislative functions, being associated with the President not only in making treaties, but in the appointment of ambassadors, ministers, consuls, judges of the supreme court, and the other officers of the United States. From all I saw or heard of the doings of Congress, however, it appeared to me that there are very great advantages in the European plan of bringing the great ministers of state face to face with their real masters in the legislature; and I was told that the eminent American jurist, Judge Story, had serious doubts as to the expediency of the American system. By all accounts, there is no reason to believe that the latter mode secures a purer administration of the great offices of government than the European system. Independently of other obvious considerations, there seemed a want of connection and understanding between the government and the legislative bodies, and the country does not afford a sufficient supply of men of the highest statesmanship for both the ministerial and the senatorial functions, if these are not allowed to be combined in the same individual. It seems an unhappy arrangement, that if the government should require the services of such men as Mr. Douglas or Mr. Seward, the foremost members of the Senate, that body must be deprived of its greatest ornaments and ablest leaders.

Congress meets annually, on the first Monday in December, in the Capitol at Washington, a noble building, beautifully situated. This is one of the finest buildings I have ever seen. It stands at the head of an acclivity, commanding a magnificent view of the city and surrounding country, with the river Potomac, and in the midst of fine parks and gardens. The principal front is turned from the town, towards an open space, prettily laid out with trees, grass-plots, and public walks. In the middle there is a statue of Washington, with the inscription, "First in war, first in peace, first in the hearts of his countrymen." The other front faces the town, and is reached by winding walks up a grassy bank, interspersed with trees and flowers. Immediately at the foot of this bank is PENNSYLVANIA AVENUE, the principal street in Washington, of great length, with trees at the sides; and WHITE HOUSE, the President's mansion, and other government buildings at the opposite end. The Capitol is in the Corinthian style; the body of freestone, painted white; the wings, only recently constructed, of a beautiful white marble, and all exquisitely finished in every part. Rising from the middle is a huge dome, yet incomplete, but which appeared to me too large for the structure beneath. I should have supposed the building architecturally perfect, and very elegant, without the oppressive mass above it, which looks as if it would sink down and crush the edifice below it. The American flag waves over each House on the top of the building, while it is sitting, and is lowered when it adjourns, and, from the elevated position of the Capitol, it is known easily in the city when either House rises.

The Americans seem an eminently practical people, in material things at least, and nothing can be more business-like or commodious than the rooms in which their great legislative assemblies meet; while at the same time they are neat, simple, and tasteful in design. The hall in which the House of Representatives meet is an oblong of about 100 feet long by 66 broad on the floor—but 139 by 93 feet above the galleries; the Speaker's chair is at the middle of one of the longer sides, opposite the door; the clerks are at desks beneath him; and the members are arranged semicircularly in front, with a considerable space or "floor" between the clerks' and members' seats. The latter are intersected by five passages, converging towards the Speaker, so that members can easily get to or leave their seats; and those members who require elbow-room in speaking, walk up and down these passages, and sometimes even move backwards and forwards in front of the other members, between the seats, where there is ample room for such evolutions.* In the four

* This movement is probably impossible now, since desks have been introduced.

corners of the room there are tables, with chairs and writing materials, generally fully occupied by members engaged writing. There are sofas all round, where members can sit aside and converse, and space at the ends where they can walk about. I have seen two members walking up and down in one of these spaces very lovingly, like boys, the arm of one round the other's shoulder, while the latter had his arm round the waist of the former. All is free and easy in Congress. The members' seats had no desks. This was the first session in the present Hall, and the previous Congress had ordered the House to be fitted up without desks. In the old House, and in the present Senate, each member had in front of him a desk on which he could write and keep his papers under lock and key. Members, however, were found to be so busy writing, folding letters and documents to their constituents, etc., that the speakers were annoyed and little attended to, while business was greatly impeded. Accordingly, desks were voted out in the new House. But when it came to be tried, the great body of the members were dissatisfied with the new arrangement. I overheard one member speaking to a friend very violently against it, and denouncing it as "a contemptible imitation of the British Parliament." I understand that a vote of the House has since ordered the desks to be restored.

The galleries are very large and important parts of the Houses of Congress. The "sovereign people" are not to be huddled up in a corner, as in England. The walls of the body of the House rise about 12 feet, and then slope back all round for a gallery, with five rows of seats, and, in the House of Representatives, capable of containing from 1000 to 1200 people. No order is required for admission. One side is for gentlemen; another part for ladies and gentlemen with them, but I saw many ladies going unattended by any of the other sex. Other parts of the gallery are reserved for reporters, certain public officers, or special orders. When I was there, the galleries were filled mostly with ladies and gentlemen belonging, I should suppose, to the best classes in the city. It was difficult to hear in the gallery; partly, I suppose, from the construction of the House, and sometimes from the "eternal hubbub and buzzing amongst the members on the floor," as a newspaper describes it; greatly from the continual talking of the visitors, which they did not take any pains to confine to a low whisper; and there was no officer watching the auditors and commanding "silence." Indeed, the galleries on several occasions gave expression to their feelings with their hands and feet; and these interruptions rose to such a height one day, that the acting chairman had to reprove the audience, and threatened to clear the galleries if they were repeated. It appeared to me that "the gallery" was a "power" in the House, far outnumbering the members, and consisting, in large proportion, of persons of wealth, station, and intelligence, fully equal to the great body of the representatives, and superior to many of them.

The House is well lighted from the ceiling, which is flat, and may be described as one great horizontal window, with an iron frame. The lighting by night is most ingenious and effective. The lights do not appear in the House; they are placed above the ceiling, the glass of which is obscured, and give a soft, equally-diffused light through every part of the House, by which I found that small print could easily be read. The effect in the House is somewhat like twilight, or rather like that peculiar light produced during an annular eclipse of the sun, sometimes seen also in certain stages of the atmosphere, when sun and rain and clouds are struggling for mastery. In the Music Hall at Boston there is another mode of lighting from above. Innumerable jets are placed all round at the cornices, and shed an equal and pleasant light through all parts of the house, while there is no flame or glare against the eyes of the audience.

There is a corridor round the House, occupying the space under the galleries, for hats, cloaks, and umbrellas; the members do not sit with their hats on as in the British House of Commons. There is a regulation of the House to this effect: "Every member shall remain uncovered during the session of the House." The room is ventilated by numerous openings in the walls and floor, through which air is forced by a fanner, worked by a steam-engine, being suitably warmed in cold weather by steam-pipes before entering the hall.

The American legislator partakes of the activity and restlessness which characterize the nation: he is always wanting something, a newspaper, an envelope, a glass of water, to post a letter, or send a message to some one outside, etc. On first entering the House I was surprised to see a number of boys on the floor or among the seats, and to hear little cracks or pops every now and then. These flying Cupids, or *pages* as they are termed, are there to wait upon the members and supply their various wants. Spiritualism is but in its infancy, and not being yet sufficiently advanced to provide spirit-waiters, the United States legislators have at present to put up with material attendants, whom they select as like spirits, as small and light as can be had; hence the number of imps whom I saw scattered through the House. When a member wishes one of these to come to him he gives a light clap of his hands; this explained the little cracks every now and then like pop-guns going off, which puzzled me at first. The nearest pages, two, or sometimes three, fly towards the sound, and attend to his wants. When not engaged, these pages wait on the floor or lounge on the vacant seats in a quite-at-home sort of way. Young America is not encumbered with much deference for years, or superior station.

The House of Representatives is a most interesting, most lively scene. All round the House is the gallery, itself a sight, with about one thousand spectators, including numbers of the "beauty and fashion," and highest intelligence of the city. On the floor below are upwards of two hundred chosen guardians of the destinies of an empire nearly as large as Europe, ostensibly seeking the interests of one common country, but separated into two hostile camps, the fiery sons of the South, indignant that their "State sovereignty" and peculiar institution should be interfered with; and the ardent "sons of liberty" from the North, impatient of the dark stain on the great republic—all impulsive, excitable, animated, and all gifted with an intolerable power of talk. Every spot of that floor has something going on. In the corners are members busy with all their might, writing, folding, sealing, with attendant imps waiting their orders. On the sofas all round are representatives, conversing, reading, lolling in every attitude; and the spaces at the ends and near the door are filled with groups talking, or more restless spirits walking up and down. Pop, pop, go the signals for the pages, and away they fly across the floor and among the seats to answer the summons. Perhaps a "bore" has possession of the House—a forest of newspapers appears; the legislators can't waste their time listening to his prosing; so he makes his speech to the Speaker, the reporters, and the public; probably it is mere "Buncombe"* for his constituents. A member worth

* A member for a place called Buncombe, on one occasion made a strange rigmarole sort of speech not quite in harmony with his supposed sentiments. His friends next day remarked upon it, saying they did not understand what

attending to rises; down go the papers and all
eyes are fixed on him. He requires room, so
takes his place at the corner of one of the passages, and a page brings him a little table on
which he has a glass of water, and his documents, for he is going to demolish some one.
He walks down the passage towards the Speaker
and up again, across amongst the seats, and
with energetic action, never hesitating for a
word or a thought, denounces the gross inconsistency of an antagonist (for that is very often
the subject of discourse), and having crushed
him by recalling some of his former sayings or
doings, turns triumphantly towards him, with
"How do you like that record, my friend?"—
But "my friend," or "the distinguished gentleman," as they often term each other, is ready
with his answer, "to balance the account," as
he says. He explains the apparent inconsistency, and soon carries the war into the enemy's
camp. He does not need to walk up and
down; his energy gets vent in flinging his arms

he would be at. "Ah," said he, "I don't wonder at that;
I did not understand it very well myself; *it was meant for
Buncombe*," so "Buncombe" means a speech in the House
designed more particularly to wheedle the constituents of the
orator—a sop to Cerberus. There is much Buncombe in
North America.

about; now he has one hand down in his pocket, shaking the other with closed fist in the air; now both hands are plunged deep into his pockets; now he tosses his arms up above his head; and with most effective, and not ungraceful action, arrests the attention of the House. He has piqued and roused the opposite party, and the moment he has finished, a dozen spring up to reply to him. The whole proceedings are characterized by intense fire, energy, and animation.

While the House of Representatives in many respects appears so stirring and lively, compared with the British House of Commons, in one point it is dull and lifeless, compared with the latter. There is no "hear-hearing," no cheering. Every speech is listened to in silence, and concludes in silence; a laugh, when an occasion for that arises, is the only audible sign of interest given by the House. The orator is never helped on by the encouraging "Hear, hear," of a supporter, nor annoyed by the sarcastic "Hear, hear," of an opponent. His happy hits are not rewarded by "loud cheers," nor his peroration received with "great and long-continued cheering." There is a regulation of the House against any signs of approval or disapproval. This is rendered necessary by the presence of the vast crowd in the gallery that could not be restrained from sympathizing were the House to cheer, which would not be convenient. So both are forbidden to applaud, or utter any sign. Singular enough, while the House generally adheres to the regulation, the gallery does not. Again and again I heard them applauding. The House usually winks at their breach of the rule, for *vox populi* is considered *vox Dei* in the United States, and must be treated respectfully. Some strange contests at times take place between members tenacious of the dignity of the House and the gallery. Though often threatened, it is exceedingly rare that the visitors in the galleries are punished for their disorderly conduct by being turned out. This was done lately in the Senate in consequence of the conduct of the gallery, at the conclusion of Mr. Benjamin's animated secession speech. " As Mr. Benjamin concluded his speech he was greeted with uproarious applause. All over the galleries there were shouts and cheers, and waving of handkerchiefs and hurrahs, and the greatest confusion and excitement prevailed all over the House." Mr. Mason moved that the galleries be instantly cleared, which was received with hisses and whistlings in the galleries; but the motion was carried and put into execution, the first time for a number of years. The following instances in which the galleries carried the day occurred lately, the first in the Senate, the second in the House of Representatives:—

"Mr. WIGFALL: I tell you that cotton is king. (Laughter in the galleries.)

"Cries of order.

"The PRESIDENT said: The Sergeant-at-Arms will clear the gallery if it occurs again.

"Mr. HALE (rep.), of N. H., said: Mr. President, that threat was made one, two, or three times yesterday. Now is the time to carry it out.

"Order was restored.

"Mr. WIGFALL said if the exhibition of feeling in the galleries occurs again, the galleries shall be cleared, and once being cleared, we will proceed. I trust the Senate will act upon it. Decency is looked for.

"Mr. DAVIS (opp.), of Mississippi, arose from his seat, and said: I hope the Senate will be permitted to proceed. I think we attach too much importance to the expression of the galleries. I take it for granted that those warned yesterday didn't repeat it to-day. Yesterday there was one set, to-day there is a new set.

We will get them all instructed after a while. (Tremendous approval from the galleries and laughter from the senators.)"

Probably Mr. Davis had some fair friends in the gallery whom he desired to save from being turned out. The following occurred at the close of an eloquent passage in a speech by Mr. John Cochrane:—

"(General and hearty applause throughout the visitors' galleries, and partial applause from members on the floor.)

"Mr. GARNETT (opp.), of Va: I trust, Mr. Speaker, in considering a matter of such great importance, that the deliberations of this House will be allowed to proceed without interruption, whether from this floor or from the galleries. If not, I will call upon the chair to check all manifestations of applause from the galleries. Should the interruption be repeated, I will move to have the galleries cleared. (Hissing from the galleries.)

"Mr. GARNETT continued, excitedly: I now move, as a matter of self-respect, and as due to the dignity of this House, that the galleries be cleared. (Hissing more general.)

Mr. GARNETT, more excitedly: This is disgraceful, sir. Those blackguards in the gallery— (Hisses)—while violating the rule of the House, insult the dignity which is due to the representatives of the Confederacy, and I move that they be expelled from the galleries.

" Mr. Garnett while speaking pointed to the north gallery, which was full of strangers at the time. On concluding his remarks he was again assailed with a chorus of hisses.

" Mr. Lamar (opp.), of Mississippi, said it was not strange to hear hissing in the House. The same had been heard in Eden.

" The Speaker appealed to the people in the galleries to preserve order."

When I was present the House of Representatives was debating as to the election of a speaker, the clerk occupying the chair. This debate, with innumerable ballots for the officer to be chosen, continued for seven or eight weeks, no real business being done during all that time. In the election of a speaker, as in that of a president, the person chosen must have a majority of all the votes given; it is not enough that he has a greater number of votes than any other candidate; he must have more than all the others taken together; this is a *majority* vote; to decide by choosing him who has merely the greatest number of votes is called a *plurality* vote. For example, if a hundred votes are recorded, the person chosen must have at least fifty-one votes, a majority of the hundred. If no one has that number, no one is chosen, and another vote has to be taken. In the session 1859-60, which was the first of the thirty-sixth Congress, the House, as usual, met on the first Monday in December; a succession of gentlemen from different sides were proposed, and it was not till the first of February, on the forty-fourth ballot, that a speaker was at last chosen. Of the 237 members of the House three were absent, and one, the gentleman appointed, did not vote. The votes stood as follows :—

Whole number voting	233
Necessary for a choice......... 117	
Mr. Pennington	117
Mr. M'Clernand	85
Mr. Gilmer	16
Scattering (for several others)	15
	— 233

Mr. Pennington, the gentleman chosen, was a new member of the House; but that does not matter in North America, where anybody is ready for any office at five minutes' notice. The Republican, or Anti-slavery party had 113 votes in the House; ninety-three were pro-slavery and supporters of the administration; the remainder were also pro-slavery, but opponents of the government, and many of them desired a speaker who would give his influence against the government; the pro-slavery party being thus divided, they could not unite upon a speaker; but by the majority-voting rule they prevented the largest united party carrying their man. Sometimes, when it is seen that no one has any reasonable prospect of commanding a *majority*, the plurality rule is adopted at last, when he is chosen who has a greater number of votes than any other. This was not the first time that the business of Congress had been retarded by delay in the choice of a speaker. On one occasion there were 133 ballots, extending over nine weeks, before the House succeeded in obtaining a speaker, and then by the plurality rule; this was at the opening of the thirty-fourth Congress, in 1855, and I think a speaker was not chosen till after a fortnight, at the beginning of the thirty-fifth Congress.

The selection of the speaker is a point of no small party importance, as he has the appointment of all the committees, " unless otherwise specially directed by the House." This throws considerable power into the speaker's hands. A member, in recommending Mr. Sherman, said that " Mr. S. was a friend to the protection of domestic industry, and would so organize the committees as to secure the fair consideration of that question." And another member said, "If we aided in electing a democrat to the speakership, would we have a chance of exposing the frauds of the administration? I would not *say* that any gentleman occupying that chair would fix the committees so as not to expose the administration; but, from what I know of the democratic party, I rather think they would." (Shouts of laughter.)

The difficulty of finding a speaker arose out of the interminable slavery question; on that subject parties were in a state of great irritation. The mad attempt of John Brown to raise a slave insurrection at Harper's Ferry, in Virginia, was but of recent occurrence, and had excited a strong feeling of resentment amongst the slave-owners and their party. There was a general disposition in the Southern States, and not without some foundation, to attribute Brown's insane excitement on the subject of slavery to the violent writings and speeches of the abolition party. Some went further, and accused several of the republican party of being implicated in the Brown raid; but, on inquiry, these charges were not supported. A Mr. Sherman was at first proposed for the office of speaker by the *Republican* or Anti-slavery party. He was vehemently opposed by the *Democratic*, or Pro-slavery, party, on account of the extreme ground he had taken in opposition to the upholders of slavery, by joining with others in recommending for general distribution a work against slavery, by H. R. HELPER. On the first day of the session Mr. CLARK, of Missouri, moved the following resolution :—

" Whereas certain members of this House, now in nomination for speaker, did indorse and recommend the book hereinafter mentioned :

" Resolved, that the doctrines and sentiments of a certain book called 'The Impending Crisis of the South : How to meet it;' purporting to have been written by one Hinton R. Helper, are insurrectionary and hostile to the domestic peace and tranquillity of the country, and that no member of this House who has endorsed and recommended it, or the compend from it, is fit to be speaker of this House."

To understand political movements in America arising out of the slavery question, we must bear in mind what I think is sometimes forgotten in this country—that slavery is recognized and supported by the constitution of the United States, and by repeated Acts of Congress ; that each State is regarded as sovereign in respect to its own domestic institutions, with which no other State, nor even Congress, has the right to interfere; that even the leaders of the anti-slavery party, however recklessly they may talk at times, distinctly abjure, in their more guarded speeches and writings, all intention of interfering with slavery in States in which it is already established; and that all humane, sober-minded, intelligent men, however averse to the system, feel that it is a subject of great delicacy indeed, surrounded by difficulties of a most perplexing character, and shrink from exciting appeals or denunciations that inevitably tend towards a servile insurrection.

Such being the state of matters, when a book on the subject of slavery was recommended for general circulation by the signatures of no less than sixty-eight members of the House of Representatives, as well as by Mr. SEWARD, a member of the Senate and leader of the Republican party, the work was necessarily subjected to a searching examination; and, as may be well conceived, a great outcry was raised by the opposite party when the book was found to be of a wild, violent, incendiary character. It is difficult to imagine how Mr. Seward, a man of taste, talents, and accomplishments, could have indorsed such a work. We should suppose that, like unlucky Mr. Sherman, he had never read it, but signed on the recommendation of others; unfortunately, however, he declared distinctly that he had read it with deep attention. The book was not deserving of the notice it received—it was rabid, shallow, and, in some parts, downright silly, by no means creditable to the Republican party. A few extracts will illustrate its character:

"The great revolutionary movement [by which the colonies declared their independence] which was set on foot in Charlotte, Mecklenburg county, North Carolina, on the 20th day of May, 1775, has not yet been terminated, nor will it be, until every slave in the United States is freed from the tyranny of his master."—

"We believe the majority of Northern people are too scrupulous. They seem to think that it is enough for them to be mere free-soilers, to keep in check the diffusive element of slavery, and to prevent it from crossing over the bounds within which it is now regulated by municipal law. Remiss in their *national* duties, as we contend, they make no positive attack on the institution in the Southern States."

"Freemen of the North! you have approached but half-way to the line of your duty; now, for your own sakes and for ours, and for the purpose of perpetuating this great republic, we ask you, in all seriousness, to organize yourselves as *one man* under the banners of liberty and to aid us in *exterminating* slavery."—

"The non-slave-holders of the South would be fully warranted in emancipating all the slaves at once, and that, too, without any compensation whatever to those who claim to be their absolute masters and owners."

"Now, chevaliers of the lash and conservators of slavery!—You have a landed estate of 173,024,000 acres, the present average market value of which is 5·34 dollars per acre; emancipate your slaves on Wednesday morning, and on the Thursday following, the value of your lands, and ours too [the non-slave-holders in the South] will have increased to an average of at least 28·07 dollars per acre."—

"For the services of the blacks from the 20th of August, 1620, up to the 4th of July, 1869—an interval of precisely two hundred and forty-eight years ten months and fourteen days, their masters, if unwilling, ought, in our judgment, to be compelled to grant them their freedom, and to pay each and every one of them at least sixty dollars cash in hand."

"Frown, sirs; fret, foam, prepare your weapons, threat, strike, shoot, stab, bring on civil war, dissolve the Union, nay, annihilate the solar system, if you will—do all this, more, less, better, worse, anything—do what you will, sirs, you can neither foil nor intimidate us; our purpose is as firmly fixed as the eternal pillars of heaven; we have determined to abolish slavery, and so help us God, abolish it we will."

Numbers 3 and 4 of the author's measures for the abolition of slavery are worthy of attention, and characteristic of the whole work.

"3rd. No co-operation with pro-slavery politicians; no fellowship with them in religion; no affiliation with them in society."

"4th. No patronage to pro-slavery merchants; no guestship in slave-waiting hotels; no fees to pro-slavery lawyers; no employment of pro-slavery physicians; no audience to pro-slavery parsons."*

We cannot wonder that the Southern members objected to being presided over by one so

* The work contained some curious and useful statistics, very damaging to the cause of slavery. The compendium, after the publicity given to the work by the proceedings in Congress, attained an enormous sale of about 140,000. The original or larger work contained matter still more objectionable in style and tendency than the compendium. The recommendation of this work by the Republican party has compromised them much as statesmen.

much their enemy, as to recommend a book of this extreme, violent, and reckless character; and they ultimately succeeded in preventing the appointment of Mr. Sherman as Speaker. On the 30th of January, he withdrew from the contest; and two days after, the House chose as speaker, Mr. Pennington, a member of the Republican party, but who was not compromised by the endorsement of any wild incendiary publications. The pertinacity with which the Republican party, for seven or eight weeks, endeavoured to force upon the House as Speaker a man obnoxious to the majority, did much to augment the bitterness between North and South, and to foster the feeling in favour of secession. Indeed, several leading men from the South declared that the appointment of Mr. Sherman would be a signal for secession.

This book, with which the Republican party had unfortunately become identified, the recent John Brown insurrection, and the slavery question generally, occupied the House when I was at Washington, and for some weeks after. The Republican party spoke little, professing great anxiety not to waste time, but to elect a Speaker and get to the business of the country; this saved them from many rather awkward explanations. I had the pleasure of hearing several very able speeches, by Messrs. Holman, John Cochrane, Davidson, and Singleton. Their general objects were to prove that the Republican party had caused the late insurrection at Harper's Ferry, that they did purpose interference with slavery in the existing States, and that their speeches tended to such interference, although they disclaimed it; and again and again a celebrated speech delivered by Mr. Seward at Rochester was referred to, in which the term "irrepressible conflict," since so often quoted, was first brought forward. That great leader of the Republican party said—" Shall I tell you what this collision means? They who think that it is accidental, unnecessary, the work of interested or fanatical agitators, and therefore ephemeral, mistake the case altogether. It is an irrepressible conflict between opposing and enduring forces, and it means that the United States must and will, sooner or later, become either entirely a slave-holding nation, or entirely a free-labour nation."—" It is the failure to apprehend this great truth that induces so many unsuccessful attempts at final compromise between the slave and free States, and it is the existence of this great fact that renders all such pretended compromises, when made, vain and ephemeral." And again—

"The interest of the white race demands the ultimate emancipation of all men. Whether that consummation shall be allowed to take effect with needful and wise precautions against sudden change and disaster, or be hurried on by violence, is all that remains for you to decide. The white man needs this continent to labour upon." This and similar speeches, have proved very embarrassing to the moderate members of the Republican party. They at once expose the party to the imputation of encouraging the slaves to rebel, and disqualify them from administering a government based upon *harmony*, where they hold there must be an *irrepressible conflict*, and upon *compromises* which they say must be *vain* and *ephemeral*.

"In my opinion," said Mr. Davidson, "he and his party have now committed the overt act, for he and they are accessories before the fact to the treason and murders committed at Harper's Ferry. And you, Northern men, who endorse the sentiments of that compendium, are responsible for its recommendation and results. Who ever heard, until this advice was given and this speech of 'irrepressible conflict' was made and circulated—who ever heard, until Seward and the Black Republicans of Congress recommended it, of any white man in the whole country who was ready to put himself at the head of an expedition for the murder of women and children, merely because they held slaves?"

The speeches of Mr. Seward were referred to for the views of the Republican party, because he was by far the ablest and most distinguished man of that body, and looked to as likely to be the next President, should his party be able to carry the election. To the surprise and disappointment of every one, Mr. Seward was passed over at the convention which nominated the Republican candidate; and Mr. Lincoln, a very different man, and comparatively unknown, was chosen. It is generally understood that the rejection of Mr. Seward was due mainly to the animosity of a busy newspaper editor, whose merits Mr. S. had failed to appreciate when he had gifts at his disposal as Governor of New York. But Mr. Lincoln, though not previously a person whose sayings or doings were noted, had given utterance to sentiments equally obnoxious to the pro-slavery party. He had said, "In my opinion it [the slavery agitation] will not cease until a crisis shall have been reached and passed. 'A house divided against itself cannot stand.' I believe this Government cannot endure permanently half slave and half free.

The opponents of slavery will arrest the further spread of it, and place it where the public mind shall rest in the belief that it is in the course of ultimate extinction; or its advocates will push it forward, till it shall become alike lawful in all the States, old as well as new— North as well as South." The same idea as Mr. Seward's "irrepressible conflict," but preceding that gentleman by some months.

Mr. JOHN COCHRANE, one of the members for the State of New York, spoke with great ability, handling delicate questions in a dignified and courteous, yet forcible style. This gentleman seems justly regarded as one of the ablest men in the House, and representing the populous, wealthy, and intelligent free State of New York, his opinions are entitled to attention. He said:

"I sympathize, sir, deeply sympathize with our friends at the South, who are now in fearful trepidation of the incendiary's torch, and of the assassin's knife, and who tremble as upon the volcano of servile insurrection. I censure and reprobate that which has occurred and is occurring all over the North, endangering the peace of the Union, and teaching rebellion to its constitution."—After referring to the recent insurrection in Virginia, and showing the tendency of the speeches and writings of the Republicans to lead to such events, he concluded, speaking for his party in the North—

"Whatever may be the suffering, politically, endured by the Southern States, they receive the assurance of our earnest sympathy. They can endure no hardship of which we will not willingly partake; nor can we enjoy prosperity which they shall not share. We are one in interest, one in lineage, one in faith. The same organic law shields and one equal power protects us all. Such is the language of the democracy of the North to the democracy of the South. Though attached to our own local customs, we will respect those of yours, opposed though they are to our habits and usages; and whenever your rights, secured by our common constitution, are threatened or invaded, ten thousand Northern swords will flame for their defence, and Northern bayonets will bristle upon Southern plains in defence of Southern rights."

Mr. SINGLETON, one of the members for the State of Mississippi, gave a very lucid view of the state of the slavery question, and in respect to secession spoke as follows:—

"The position taken by the Republican party on this floor, of excluding slavery from all the territories which now belong to us, or which may hereafter be acquired, and their determination to repeal the fugitive slave law, will, if persevered in, sooner or later prove the destruction of every tie which binds us together. If you imagine that the people of the South will submit to be confined to their present area, to be shut out from the common territories acquired by the common blood and treasure of the nation, that slavery will linger out a poor and miserable existence within its present borders, and that our slaves are to escape without a law to recover them, I tell you to-day that you may begin to prepare for a dissolution of the Union. Every man upon this floor will counsel their constituents—though they need not be counselled—to that effect. Their determination is fixed and unalterable, that they will have an expansion of slave territory in this Union if you will allow it, or outside of the Union, if they must. Upon the supposition that the gentleman from Iowa speaks the sentiments of the Black Republican party, and that their purpose is fixed to exclude us for ever from the territories and confine us to our present limits, and that the fugitive slave law is to be repealed or so altered as to render it inefficient, if you desire to know my counsel to the people of

Mississippi, it is, that they take measures immediately, in conjunction with other Southern States, to separate from you." (Dec. 1859.)

The following pleasant dialogue took place between this gentleman and another member.

Mr. Singleton.—" Whenever gentlemen undertake to play that game with us [to chastise the South] they will find us ready for them. There is not a boy ten years old in the State of Mississippi who does not know how to handle the shot-gun and rifle. Whenever you undertake to speak of chastisement, just let us know what you mean, and we will engage to take care of ourselves."

Mr. Kilgore.—" I repeat that I did not use the word in an offensive sense; but permit me to say to the gentleman, that an acquaintance with the use of the shot-gun and the rifle is not restricted to the South. They were the toys of my youth and tools of my trade, with which I in part earned my living in after days."

Mr. Singleton.—" Well; I hope that when the time comes round, and you undertake to chastise us, you will come down with your shot-gun. I would advise you, however, not to encumber yourself too much; because, in your flight, you might want to get rid of all unnecessary articles."

Mr. KILGORE.—"I would say to the gentleman, I am not one of the artillery that flies from danger."

Mr. SINGLETON.—"Well, we will see when you come down South. We shall then be able to test you."

Mr. KILGORE.—"But I am not going South." (Laughter.)

A Mr. ANDERSON, of Kentucky, had been questioned and his conduct sharply criticised by a colleague, member for the same district. At the close of his reply, Mr. Anderson said, "Permit me, in good humour, to say a word to my colleague who has interrogated me. He has a right to do it, and I am perfectly willing to respond; but I will tell him one thing, that I once heard of a man in Virginia, in the Western part of the State, who made a very large fortune by attending to his own business (great laughter); and I heard of another man, in the Eastern part of Virginia, who made a large fortune by letting other people's business alone (renewed laughter). So far as I am concerned, I am responsible to my constituents, and not to my worthy colleague."

Although, as is well known, and might be expected in such a country, with so many irritating public questions, there are violent outbursts at times, it appeared to me that the general tone of the debates was good-humoured and gentlemanly.

An interesting occurrence took place in the House on the day on which a Speaker was at last chosen. The proceedings were opened with prayer by a Jew. The following is the newspaper notice:—

"IMPRESSIVE ADDRESS TO THE THRONE OF GRACE.—The proceedings were opened with prayer by RABBI RAPHAEL. It abounded with fervently-expressed patriotic and religious sentiment. He implored the Divine blessing to direct the House in the election of a Speaker who may preside without favour and fear, and that the members might speak and act for the glory and happiness of their common country. The prayer was listened to with marked attention."

There was no regular chaplain till after the Speaker was chosen; but the daily proceedings in the House were opened with a short prayer, by clergymen of different religious communions. The officiating minister takes his place at the side of the Speaker or President, and the members stand during the prayer. Afterwards a chaplain was appointed, with a salary of 750 dollars for the session. Some members expressed a wish that ministers of all denominations should be invited, to officiate alternately; and one moved to postpone the election till the 1st of July (when Congress usually has adjourned). A great number were proposed, and among them the Rabbi Raphael; but his name and the names of several others were withdrawn before the votes were taken, and, after one or two ballots, a Mr. Stockton was chosen.

In the month of January, 1860, a curious passage at arms took place between a member of the House of Representatives and the *New York Herald*. In consequence of some remarks in the paper which gave offence to the member, whom we shall call Mr. Z., he favoured the House with a very pungent sketch of the character of the proprietor of the *Herald*, whom he painted as very black, indeed, and made some very strong statements, which, even if true, one would be very reluctant to publish of any one. The *Herald* took its revenge in the following original manner. In the reports of the debates of the three days following Mr. Z.'s attack, short notices were interpolated, such as the following:—

X. Y. Z. The filthy liar and libeller of —— [the State he represented] said nothing.

Then, after the reports of various speeches—

X. Y. Z., etc., as before, made no remark.

X. Y. Z., etc., made no speech to-day.

X. Y. Z., the shameless liar and calumniator of ——, did not open his mouth.

X. Y. Z., the brutal liar and slanderer of ——, did not say a word.

Thirteen times were these elegant compliments repeated, with the member's name in full. A member of the House brought forward a motion to expel the reporters of the *Herald*, who, it was admitted, had nothing to do with the offensive interpolations; but the matter dropped. It was remarked by another member that "The official organ of the administration, the *Constitution*, had so far forgotten its dignity as to stigmatize the Republicans as traitors, using language foul and loathsome, and saying they had been bought with a shilling. If the axe is to fall, let it fall on all libellers. He was a friend of freedom of the press, and if gentlemen do not like the press to strike back, they should themselves withhold the blow."

It would be unjust to let it be understood that these are fair specimens of the American press; they are quite exceptional. There may be, in the United States, a few papers that use coarse language and an offensive style, but the great majority of the newspapers are conducted in a respectable manner. We do not see the best class of United States papers in this country. To those desiring to take an American paper (and a good one is full of interesting matter), I should recommend the weekly edition of the Boston Courier, on the Democratic side, and the weekly edition of the New York Evening Post, on the Republican side. These are large papers, price four cents (twopence) each, with few advertisements, a great amount of well selected and interesting general reading, able articles on the news of the day, and conducted with taste as well as talent. The distinguished poet, W. C. Bryant, is the chief proprietor of the *Post*.

Congress has a peculiar method of providing reports of the debates, which has been pleasantly described by a member as one of the wonders of the world. The proprietors of the *Globe*, at Washington, have a grant for executing this work, and publish two editions—a *Daily Globe*, and one in quarto, called the *Congressional Globe*, which is the authorised edition, the American "Hansard." It seems very difficult to report proceedings in Congress, in consequence, I suppose, of the noise and disorder that prevail; accordingly, the reporters avail themselves of the assistance of members, to get correct accounts of what has been said and done, and the members avail themselves of the opportunity to improve and polish their orations, and prune off any exuberances that don't look very well next morning. One gentleman objected strongly to appropriating money to publish speeches which are never made. He said that it is well known that the speeches that are published in the *Globe* are not the speeches that are delivered upon the floor of the House; that members constantly go and strike out what they please, and put in what they think best on second consideration. He stated further, that he had sometimes gone to revise what he had said in putting a question, or replying to one, and found next morning that others had gone too, and had struck out from their speeches the parts that had called forth his remarks, so that they appeared in the *Globe* without meaning of any kind. Members don't always confine themselves to correcting their own speeches; they sometimes strike out anything unpleasant they may see in an adversary's. In a notable instance connected with a challenge, which strangely did *not* lead to a duel, one member admitted having done this. "I erased no word which *the reporter* had written upon his manuscript, but I felt myself authorised to erase an unwarrantable and impertinent interpolation in the gentleman's own handwriting." He was determined the objectionable interpolation should not appear, for he erased it so effectually that neither reporters nor printers could tell what were the words which had been written. The *Globe* is almost the only paper in which one finds full and readable reports of the proceedings in Congress. Some New York papers give them at considerable length, but in print so small and close, that it is a painful effort, even for strong eyes, to wade through them. The greater number of papers give summaries, with now and then a notable speech in full.

There is one of the usages of Congress which seems to have considerable advantages, and an aspect of fairness, while it is certainly a proof that the "tyranny of the majority" does not prevail everywhere in American institutions. When a committee of either House is not unanimous, the minority may, if they think proper, also present a report, and this is very generally done with committees on important questions. Sometimes the minority is divided, and then there are two or more minority reports, all of which are received, even though one of the minorities be the smallest possible—one member only.

While the debates in Congress are very animated, eloquent, and argumentative, they are by no means so instructive as those in the British Parliament. This arises, I think, greatly from the absence of the ministers of state; these are the persons possessed of the fullest and most correct information on most of the subjects of debate, and Congress not only loses the benefit of the minute and accurate knowledge which they could supply, but, unchecked by their presence, members are apt to indulge in loose, careless statements, and to speak a good deal at random. Another cause is the number of important subjects excluded from Congress by the large legislative powers left to the individual States. The proceedings in the several State legislatures are usually reported very briefly, and seem to be but little regarded. All eyes are turned intently on the great national assemblies at Washington; one parliament is quite enough to attend to; and thus, from the comparative neglect of the local parliaments, much valuable information, and many useful political lessons are lost. The American, too, has a great tendency towards declamation and oratorical effect. The British legislator is more a man of facts and figures. The latter is not only less excitable by nature than the American, but he has, generally speaking, received a much superior education, and is less in the habit of addressing popular audiences who must be excited and interested by strong statements and a frothy style. The more one sees'or hears of other assemblies, the more we must admire the British Parliament (I trust this is not mere national prejudice). A great debate in the House of Commons, or House of Lords, is truly a masterly performance, and one of the finest intellectual displays the world affords.

A new Congress is chosen every two years, and there is always a considerable number of new members, particularly from the North. When a Southern State, it was said, falls upon a good representative, it knows his value and keeps him; but the North is fond of changes. Of the present House (1859-61) of 237 members, only 112 were members of the previous Congress, a majority, 125, being new members. For a large number of members, it is a very good thing being appointed to Congress; they have £600 a year for two years, and the chances of what they may pick up at Washington. Many representatives, I heard it freely said, have been known to come to Congress poor men, and to leave it rich, or, at least, independent; especially chairmen of committees, by getting bills passed. The Government has a variety of good things to bestow, as contracts for post roads, for carrying the mails, supplying the army and navy, etc.; and the House itself has some gifts worth looking after, such as the printing for Congress. The appointment of printer is usually given to some influential party man in favour with the majority. Governor Ford was re-elected printer in 1860. The nominal printer is seldom really a printer. The spoil is considerable. He gives a little to the man who does the work, a good deal to the various jackals who have helped him to the job, and reserves the lion's share for himself. From an investigation made lately, it appears that about 100 cents have been charged to the country for work that respectable printers offered to do for from seven to fourteen cents.

On the recent national fast day, one clergyman said in his discourse—" The crowning shame, and the damning stigma on the forefront of the Republic, is bribery. Our fathers, like Samuel, could call God and the people to witness that no bribe had ever blinded their eyes to pervert judgment; while their degenerate sons, in the high places of the nation, in the halls of the State, and of the city, and, shall I say, in the tribunals of an elective and poorly paid judiciary, are, like the sons of Samuel, charged with turning aside after lucre, and taking bribes and perverting judgment."

The Republican party allege that jobbing and corruption have been carried to a greater extent by the administration now coming to a close than by any former government: that endeavours have been made to bribe the conductors of influential newspapers and even members of Congress to procure their support. The present House of Representatives is animated by extremely hostile feelings towards Mr. Buchanan, arising mainly out of the support he has given to the pro-slavery party in Kansas, and his efforts to force slavery upon that new State, in opposition, as it is said, to the wishes of the *bonâ fide* settlers. They made two grand attacks upon him last session. By a majority of 117 to 45, a committee was appointed to inquire " whether the President of the United States, or any other officer of the government, has, by money, patronage, or other improper means, sought to influence the action of Congress, or any committee thereof, for or against the passage of any law appertaining to the rights of any State or territory, and whether the President has failed or refused to compel the execution of any law thereof"— referring to the charge that he had not used means in his power to suppress the disorders in Kansas. Mr. Buchanan sent to the House two energetic protests against such an investigation, on the grounds that the House has no authority to take any steps against the President unless by impeachment, for which a proper court, presided over by the chief justice, has been appointed; that Mr. Covode, the mover of the committee, and his accuser, becomes one of his judges; that in former cases of inquiry, the subject was referred to a standing committee, the judiciary committee, appointed without reference to any special case; and that the inquiry was vague and general, without any specific charge;—he said that since the times of the Star-Chamber and of general warrants, there had been no such proceeding in England, and that he had a right to be informed in the beginning of the nature of the accusation against him. But the House held that it was not an accusation, but an inquiry, and that they had a right to inquire into the proceedings of the government. The committee unfolded some very strange doings in the course of their inquiry, but I do not understand that they suc-

I

ceeded in implicating the President. The session closed before there was time to act on the report; but, ostensibly on another ground, the House passed a vote of censure on the President, to the effect that "the Secretary of the Navy has, with the sanction of the President, abused his discretionary power in the selection of a coal agent, and for the purchase of fuel for the government,"—"that the distribution of the patronage of the navy yards among members of Congress is destructive of discipline and injurious to the public service; that the President and the Secretary of the Navy, in considering the party relations of bidders and the effect of awarding contracts pending elections, are deserving of the reprobation of this House." These resolutions were carried by a majority of 120 to 65. But when all the circumstances are considered, the proceeding has somewhat of the aspect of the " tyranny of a majority"— for they were the resolutions of a *minority* of a committee of the *previous Congress* appointed to inquire and report on the subject, and were rejected by the committee which made the investigation; while resolutions of an opposite character were carried and reported to the House. The rejected resolutions were now raised from the dead and brought forth to annoy the President and Secretary of the Navy.

The office of member of Congress being so desirable a thing, there are many who aspire to it, and the constituency not being very select, nor very stable or consistent, are easily persuaded to give their votes for a new man who has been undermining the present possessor. New faces and new promises have charms for the mob. The absent are always in the wrong; besides, are they not very well off?—they have had it already for two years, or four years, and so-and-so should have a chance now! Fortunately, the Senate is chosen upon a different system. Its members are selected by, perhaps, the highest, most intelligent constituency the State can furnish—the State Legislature; and its members once chosen, retain their office for six years. The Senate is the Conservative element in the Constitution of the United States—the only drag upon the wheel of revolution, which has a constant tendency to be in motion in the Great Republic. It is worthy of remark that this body, chosen by a constituency of high standing, contains many of the ablest and most high-minded and independent men of the nation; which cannot be said either of the representatives or of the presidents, who are the choice of universal suffrage. The first few presidents, Washington, Adams, Jefferson, really were men of mark—the foremost men of the time. But when we study the history of the United States during the last thirty or forty years, we find Clay, Calhoun, Webster, Cass, Everett, Douglas, Seward, in the front rank on every trying occasion, distinguished above all others by their talents, their high character and standing, and their great public services—but we do not find their names in the list of presidents. Of these able and eminent statesmen, one asks, Why have they never been elevated to the dignity of president? Of the majority of the presidents of the last forty years, it is asked, Why have they been elevated to this office? There is one answer to both questions. Because of the ignorance of a universal suffrage constituency, and of the charlatanism and petty jealousies of those who guide it.

In America, including the British Colonies, a large proportion of men of the highest class—of those eminently fitted to be useful, faithful, and judicious public servants—stand aloof from politics. Some shrink from subjecting themselves to the rough, coarse, turbulent treatment which public men must there undergo; others stand back on account of the uncertainty attending public offices, some held by law for only short periods, and all dependent directly or indirectly on the caprice of popular elections. In Britain we have, fortunately, a large class of gentlemen of independent means, willing to serve their country for no other object than the gratification of a natural and harmless ambition or the laudable desire to be useful: and we have not (and I trust never will have) the wretched systems of elections for short periods and turning out every one on a change of Government. This independent class is very small in North America, and, small as it is, numbers of it are deterred by the prevalent system from entering into public life. Popular election and the short period of office deprive the American Governments of the services of the majority of the ablest and most honourable men in the State; men of an inferior stamp, noisy, ranting, shallow, trading politicians, get possession of place and power; the Government is vulgarized, corrupted, demoralized, and the nation with it. The following is from a Boston paper: "We heard a well-informed citizen, the other day, reply to the question why a very desirable candidate was not appointed to a foreign mission of importance, by saying, he had three great disqualifications — first, he was a gentleman;

secondly, he was an accomplished scholar and statesman; and thirdly, he was an honest man." This great evil is felt in the British Colonies and in the State Legislatures of the United States, as well as in Congress; the latter, however, in so large and populous a country, must attract a considerable amount of talent, at least; while the Senate always contains several men of great abilities and high standing.

It is sad to see, as one often does in America, men of the highest class, who have deserved well of their country, cast aside and deprived of the station and honours which would gratify their legitimate ambition, and solace the evening of their days, and to which, by superior talents and accomplishments, and a long career of public usefulness, they had a natural right to look forward; while far inferior, and sometimes quite obscure persons, are preferred, and thrust into offices which they degrade;—but such are the cruel disappointments which await the most gifted and high-minded men under the rough democratic system of North America.

I visited Congress several times, and have since paid some attention to its proceedings. When we think on the peculiar and unfavourable circumstances of large tracts of that young country that must still furnish members to

Congress, we cannot but admire the singular ability and legislative capacity exhibited by the two assemblies. Very few, indeed, of the members have had educational advantages at all to be compared with those enjoyed by the great majority of the British legislators; but the general diffusion of a sound elementary education, with the intellectual habits and natural genius of the people, make up, to a considerable extent, for the want of this higher early culture. It is true, there is much unprofitable talk, and much empty declamation; we hear now and then of short-comings, irregularities, and occasional manifestations of the all-prevailing rowdyism; and we, in Britain, are accustomed to a more sober, quiet, decorous style of proceeding. But Rome was not built in a day. Few governments have a right to boast of unmixed success in their mission, and Europe has not exhibited many national assemblies that can be held forth as models. The elements of constitutional government are there; there are the representative system, and the responsibility of the rulers to the nation in full action (though that responsibility is not due exactly to the best class of society). They derived these institutions from us; the two peoples should sympathize with each other, for they stand alone amongst the nations, distinguished by the large measure of freedom which they enjoy, and by the possession of those glorious instruments for the preservation of freedom—Congress and Parliament. With all their faults, where, on the face of the earth, can we find their equal? Congress has now flourished for a period of eighty years; her system has many imperfections, but time will make them be felt, and suggest remedies. Her greatest trials are probably yet to come; but when we think of the talent, information, and sagacity, exhibited in the two Houses, of the intelligence of the great body of the people, of the ingenuity, fertile resources, and practical character of the nation in other respects, we are led to hope that the difficulties will be surmounted, and freedom and good government be permanently secured to this great and most interesting people.

A few specimens of speeches and proceedings in Congress may be interesting. The first extract is from the speech of Mr. HALE, a Republican member for New Hampshire:—

" We are trying an experiment, and I believe we are in its crisis. I have never been of that number of Fourth of July orators who glorify the country. I have uniformly said we are but in the beginning of an experiment. We talk of our republic. Why, sir, it has not outlived the ages of the soldiers who fought its battles and gained its victories. I believe Rome existed as a republic for 600 years. That is something to be proud of. But we have not survived a lifetime of the men who fought the battles of liberty, or the patriots and sages who formed our constitution and government. We have obtained what we have obtained by great effort and at great price. It was not the mere price of the revolution, or the mere price of the blood that was shed, or the patriot counsels that formed the constitution ; but, away back, centuries upon centuries, in English history, when power and principle contended—in all those centuries there has been going on a contest which is culminating in our experiment here. No patriot blood poured out on the battle-fields of civil war in England has been insignificant in this conflict. I will add this, that we shall present a most humiliating spectacle to this world, if, at this time, when, by the acknowledgment of the President of the United States, the blessings of heaven have descended upon this people in all the channels of their industry and business—at a time when, by the confession of the senator from Georgia (Mr. Toombs) last year on this floor, this general government was faithfully performing all its functions in relation to the Slave States and every State—I say, under such circumstances of a faithful government, and I will add, of a subservient judiciary, if this confederacy should burst, and this glorious community of States be dissevered and fail, by the doubtful contingency of State action, to carry out the experiment of human liberty; and when at the very day and hour that we are coming to such a result, the States of Italy, having for centuries gone through a baptism of blood, and been taught by the despotism of centuries, are coming together to unite their energies for liberty and progress; then, if we, untaught by all the past, and reckless of the present, and blind to the future, should madly dash ourselves upon this dark ocean, whose shores no eye of prophecy or faith can discern, I do not know what is to be the future."

The following is an illustration of the very strong things that are sometimes said, even in the Senate. The speaker is Mr. IVERSON, a fiery son of the South and decided Secessionist, member for the State of Georgia. The tyrant for whom a Brutus is suggested, because he opposes secession, is General Houston, the Governor of Texas.

" Though there is a clog in the way, in the lone star of Texas, in the person of the Governor, who will not consent to call the legislature, yet the public sentiment is so strong that even her Governor may be overridden; and if he will not yield to the public sentiment, some Texan Brutus may arise to rid his country of this old hoary-headed traitor. (Great sensation.) There has been a good deal of vapouring and threatening, but they came from the last men who would carry out their threats. Men talk about their eighteen millions, but we hear a few days afterwards of these same men being switched in the face, and they tremble like a sheep-stealing dog. There will be no war. The North, governed by such far-seeing statesmen as the senator from New York (Mr. Seward), will see the futility of this. In less than twelve months a Southern confederacy will be formed, and it will be the most successful government on earth. The Southern States, thus banded together, will be able to resist any force in the world. We do not expect war, but we will be prepared for it, and we are not a feeble race of Mexicans either. But he hoped the Northern States would allow them to form their government, and make friendly and commercial treaties with them. They would allow the North the advantage of a favoured nation. There was a feeling of enmity between the two sections deeper than the depths of hell. We are enemies. The Northern people, he believed, hated the South worse than England hated France, and he could tell his brethren there was no love lost between them. (Laughter in the galleries.) He thought, under all these circumstances, they had better separate. He should not have said anything, but for the remarks of the senator from New Hampshire, who threatened war as if to frighten the South. 'War is inevitable. Let the South take care.' Let the war come, and we will meet the senator from New Hampshire and all the myrmidons of abolitionism, and, in the language of the honourable representative from Ohio (Mr. Corwin), in regard to the Mexican war, we will 'welcome them with bloody hands to hospitable graves.' (Sensation.)"

Next follow some of the ideas of Mr. DANIEL SICKLES, a member of the House of Representatives for New York; the same who killed Mr. Key, in Washington, in the spring of 1859.

" One of these delusions is that disunion can be prevented by force ; that the Union can by revolution be brought to the verge of destruction, yet at the last that the strong arm of power can stay the work. On the call for force, come whence it may, no man would pass the frontier of the city of New York to wage war against a State which, through its constituted authority, should, for its rights, interests, and honour, seek safety in a separate existence. The Union can be made perpetual by justice, but not by force; and if these truths were engraved on the hearts of the people of the North and the East and the West, all would be well. Until these truths are recognized there cannot be peace. The city of New York will cling to the Union while a single hope is left; but when there is no longer a Union, proud as she is of her position as a metropolis, ready to banish sectional prejudices, and willing to contribute all in her power to maintain her honour at home and abroad—when there is no longer a Union, she will never consent to be an appendage or slave of a Puritan Province. She will assert her own independence. There is no sympathy now between the city and State of New York, nor has there been for years. She will open her free port to the commerce of the world."

The proceedings of the House of Representatives are sometimes enlivened in a way that rather startles us sober Britishers a little, but is not thought much of amongst a people at once so excitable and so free and easy. A few reports of such scenes are subjoined, not that they are frequent, or interfere materially with the performance of a vast amount of useful work, but because they illustrate the present condition of things in America, and are characteristic of Brother Jonathan :—

" During the speech some one sent Mr. Smith a tumbler of egg nogg, which he drank, saying, ' Merry Christmas to all of you.' (Great laughter.)

" Mr. KILGORE inquired whether it was in order for the gentleman to monopolize the drinking of egg nogg, while the rest were doing without it?

" Mr. SMITH said that was one of the constitutional privileges of his side of the House. (Laughter.)

" A VOICE.—I'd like to have some; I'm dry as thunder. (Loud ' ha, ha's ' all over the House.)

" After further remarks Mr. Smith received another tumbler of egg nogg, which he drank, bowing to the ladies in the galleries, creating much merriment.

"Mr. Burnett.—I rise to a question of privilege. I desire to know whether this is a private treat or not? (Laughter.)

"Mr. Moore, of Ky. (earnestly)—I move to adjourn to take some kind of treat. (Increased laughter.)

"The Clerk.—I do not feel authorized to decide, but will submit the question to the House. (Renewed laughter.)"

* * * * *

"In the Senate he reiterated that the Homestead bill constituted a part of the Republican platform.

"Mr. Pugh.—Where do you find it in the Republican platform?

"Mr. Wigfall—(pointing to Mr. Seward and Lord Lyons, who were talking together on one of the sofas).—There it is, talking to Lord Lyons. The British Minister and the platform are together.

"Mr. Pugh.—I deny that the Republican platform says anything about the Homestead bill. They have only taken it up, according to their habit of picking up whatever they find lying about loose.

"Mr. Wigfall apologized for referring to gentlemen by name, and then continued his remarks, which were of a very discursive character." * * * *

"Mr. HASKIN asked if Clark agreed to this programme. Clark replied at once, 'It's none of your business.' Haskin was greatly provoked, and was proceeding to make some statements respecting his colleague, when he was called to order (he was not at that time entitled to the floor) very vehemently by the democratic members. In his violent gesticulations Mr. Haskin unfortunately dropped a pistol from his coat-pocket. He hastily replaced it in his coat, but the action was seen by several Southern democrats, who supposed that he was about to use it. Then ensued a scene which defies description. For several minutes a collision seemed inevitable, but the Sergeant-at-Arms and a score of peacemakers at last produced quiet. Mr. Haskin then made an explanation, Mr. Clark an apology, and the House adjourned. Clemens, of Virginia, seemed disposed to condemn Mr. Haskin for bringing a pistol into the House; but he must have been aware that, at that moment, there were probably not five Southern members in the House who were not armed."
* * * * *

"The Avenue presented a very gay and animated scene, from the number of beautifully-dressed ladies, who, even then, with two hours before them, showed their anxiety not to be behind time.

"At this moment the doorkeepers are expelling gentlemen from the ladies' galleries, and the greatest excitement prevails—as, whenever one of the lords shows fight, the ladies come to the assistance of the doorkeepers, and, as many hands make light work, of course the refractory disappears amid the tumultuous uproar of the galleries. The pages below are reaping a harvest from fallen jewellery. One shower, to the right of the Speaker's chair, called forth a regular scramble among the crowds who were perambulating the chamber, and some funny falls and tumbles over were the result.

"Very few members have as yet taken their seats. They stand in groups on the right and left. There is a general move below, and a few favoured ladies are shooting across (in the body of the House), like birds skimming over a lake, to a point where seats have been placed for them. The gentlemen who are not entitled to seats upon the floor are slowly retiring before the officers, and something like order is beginning to appear from the late chaos.

"The gavel strikes, and silence is restored,

K

as the chaplain takes his stand. Rev. Mr. Kennard, in the course of his prayer, implored the Almighty to come to the deliverance of the country from its present excitement and danger, and to renew the bond of confidence which formerly existed as to our confederacy.

"It is a few minutes to one o'clock, and the greatest confusion prevails. Half a dozen members from the Democratic benches are up at once, in fearful excitement, speaking to questions of order, and creating the most dreadful disorder. A motion is before the House for the exclusion of the unprivileged from the floor.

"Mr. JOHN COCHRANE, as a question of 'high privilege,' moves that the ladies on the floor be excepted. While this question is yet undecided, Mr. Smith, of Virginia, in gratitude to the sex, a merry member of which, it is said, sent him the famous glass of egg nogg, is busy providing seats for such as are pressing uncomfortably upon the doorkeeper. There is a half circle of them now seated on the Republican side of the House, but an ample skirt here and there at the doors, and a half-dozen faces glowing bright in the background, give note of the anxious crowd who are yet unprovided for, and Mr. Ashmore, making himself heard above the din that reigns around, calls upon the Clerk to enforce the orders of the House. 'Is this,' he asks, 'a dignified body—a respectable body of men? No, Mr. Clerk, we are a mob—nothing but a mob.' A hearty confirmatory response is given from the galleries all round. ' If you intend to enforce the orders of the House in part, say so; but if you extend the same courtesy to all the ladies alike, throw open the doors, and give seats to the wives and daughters of those members who are yet excluded.' (Cries of 'Good, good,' from the galleries.)

"Mr. OLIN (Rep.), of N. Y., reminded gentlemen that we have no rules.

"Mr. SMITH, of Va., replied—We have the parliamentary law.

"After a debate the floor was cleared of the ladies, and many unprivileged persons of the other sex, and the House decided to proceed to a ballot."

* * * * *

"The session of the House last night was a very stormy one, and it was very fortunate that Mr. Dawes, of Massachusetts, was in the chair. Mr. Pennington would have been trodden under foot by the tumult, but Mr. Dawes held the reins of government with a firm grasp, and neither bullying nor coaxing would make him swerve a hair to the right or left. A great many strangers were upon the floor—delegates to the Baltimore Convention—where they had no right, and they added very much to the confusion. Martin, of Virginia, in a very loud voice, begged the Speaker to make the doorkeeper do his duty and clear the floor of the strangers; but the officer of the House found it impossible, without resorting to force, to execute the order of the House, and many of them remained."

* * * * *

On Thursday, in the House, Mr. Lovejoy, of Illinois, in Committee of the Whole, nominally on the tariff, maintained that polygamy was no worse than slavery, and that both were twin relics of barbarism. The report gives the following account of the close of the discussion on that day:—

"Mr. Lovejoy, who had commenced his remarks on the extreme left of the Republican side, had gradually advanced into the space in front of the Speaker's chair, and, as he warmed in his subject, he began to gesticulate with some vehemence. He was interrupted by Mr. Pryor, of Va. (Dem.), who excitedly called him to order, at the same time advancing towards him with fierce gesticulations. He was understood to say, prefacing the remark with some offensive adjectives, 'Keep your own side, sir; you shall not come over here, shaking your fists in the faces of gentlemen!'

"Great confusion ensued. Members began to rush towards the scene from all sides, some shouting order, and others denouncing Lovejoy.

"Mr. PRYOR.—I call him to order, sir. He shall not shake his fists in our faces, sir. It is bad enough to let him stand over there and talk his treason.

"Mr. BARKSDALE, of Mississippi (Dem.), who had been in his seat with a heavy cane in his hand, came forward with the crowd, shouting and flourishing the cane. The only words understood from him above the din of the Chairman's gavel, were, 'Keep his own side, the rascal.'

"Mr. ADRAIN, of New Jersey (Anti-Lecompton Dem.), and other gentlemen, moved that the Committee rise; and some called the Sergeant-at-Arms.

"The Chairman would receive no motion till gentlemen resumed their seats.

"The crowd still increased, and a collision seemed inevitable.

"Mr. Cox, of Ohio (Dem.), shouted—I rise to a point of order. The gentleman from Illinois is out of his seat. He has no right to leave his seat and come upon the Democratic side.

"Mr. LOVEJOY, standing firm, was understood to reply, 'I will stand where I please.'

"He stood at this time on the Republican side near the dividing aisle."

* * * * *

"He (Lovejoy) proposed to hold up to the retribution of public sentiment slaveholding in all its atrocity and hideousness, just as gentlemen had here polygamy. Public sentiment will burn and scour out slavery, and the proper way is by the action of the Slave States themselves. He had endorsed the Helper book because he wanted to do it; he did so without asking the gentleman from Missouri (Clark), or anybody else. You shed the blood of my brother twenty years ago, and I am here, free to speak my mind. He wanted to say in Charleston what he could say here.

"Mr. BONHAM.—You had better try it!

"Mr. LOVEJOY.—I can go to England and there discuss the question of Church and State, or any other British institution. But if I go into the Slave States and talk against Slavery, where is my protection?

"Mr. MILES, of North Carolina (Dem.).— Can you go to England and incite the labouring classes there to assassinate the Queen?

"Mr. Lovejoy.—I don't desire to do that. I claim the right to discuss slavery everywhere under the stars and stripes."

* * * * *

"Every slave has a right to run away in spite of your laws, and to fight himself away. Were he (Lovejoy) a slave, and were it necessary to achieve his freedom, he would not hesitate to fill up the chasm and bridge it over with the carcases of the slain. He loved the South.

"A voice.—We don't love you."

* * * * *

"Mr. Martin, of Virginia (Dem.).—If you will come into Virginia, we will hang you higher than we did John Brown.

"Mr. Lovejoy.—No doubt about it."

Some peculiarities in the regulations of the House of Representatives are of interest.

The question is put, *ay* or *no*. Then, if the Speaker doubt, or a division be called for, the House shall divide; those in the affirmative of the question shall rise first from their seats, and afterwards those in the negative. If the Speaker still doubt, or a count be required, the Speaker shall name two members, one from each side, to tell the members in the affirmative; which being reported, he shall rise and state the decision to the House, etc. The House divides by each party rising, not by leaving the Hall. In all cases of election by the House of its officers, the vote is taken *vivâ voce*. The names are called out by the Clerk, and each member tells aloud for whom he votes.

All committees are appointed by the Speaker unless otherwise specially directed by the House, in which case they shall be appointed by ballot; and if, upon such ballot, the number required shall not be elected by a majority [see page 93] of the votes given, the House shall proceed to a second ballot, in which a plurality of votes shall prevail. In all other cases of ballot than for committees, a majority of the votes given shall be necessary to an election; and where there shall not be such a majority on the first ballot, the ballots shall be repeated until a majority be obtained.

After six days from the commencement of a second or subsequent session of any Congress, all bills, resolutions, and reports which originated in the House, and at the close of the next preceding session remained undetermined, shall be resumed and acted upon in the same manner as if no adjournment had taken place.

Members must confine themselves to the question under debate, and avoid personality.

No member shall occupy more than one hour in debate on any question in the House, or in Committee; but a member reporting the measure under consideration from a committee may open and close the debate: *Provided*, that where debate is closed by order of the House, any member shall be allowed, in committee, five minutes to explain any amendment he may offer, after which any member who shall first obtain the floor shall be allowed to speak five minutes in opposition to it, and there shall be no further debate on the amendment; but the same privilege of debate shall be allowed in favour of, and against any amendment that may be offered to the amendment, and neither the amendment, nor an amendment to the amendment, shall be withdrawn by the mover thereof, unless by the unanimous consent of the committee.

No member shall speak more than once to the same question without leave of the House, unless he be the mover, proposer, or introducer of the matter pending; in which case he shall be permitted to speak in reply, but not until every member choosing to speak shall have spoken.

While the Speaker is putting any question, or addressing the House, none shall walk out of, or across the House; nor in such case, or when a member is speaking, shall entertain private discourse; nor while a member is speaking, shall pass between him and the chair.

Twenty-eight standing committees, of nine members each, are appointed at the beginning of each session, on the following subjects:—
1. Of nine members each: elections; ways and means; claims; commerce; public lands; post-office and post roads; the district of Columbia; the judiciary; revolutionary claims; public expenditure; private land claims; manufactures; agriculture; Indian affairs; military affairs; the militia; naval affairs; foreign affairs; the territories; revolutionary pensions; invalid pensions; roads and canals. 2. Of five members each: on patents; public buildings and grounds; revisal and unfinished business; accounts; mileage; engraving (three members).

The committee of revisal and unfinished business examines and reports what laws have expired, or are near expiring, and require to be revived or further continued; also, from the journal of last session, all such matters as were then depending and undetermined.

Six committees, of five members each, are

appointed to examine and report upon the public accounts and expenditures of the department of State, the treasury department, the department of war, the department of the navy, the post-office, and the public buildings.

A joint committee of the two Houses, of three members from each, is appointed on the public printing.

No spirituous liquor shall be offered for sale, or exhibited within the Capitol, or on the public grounds adjacent thereto.

Having been but a short time in Washington, so that I had few opportunities of acquiring information, I am aware that my account of Congress must be very imperfect. It requires time, and friends whom one can question freely, to get below the surface of things. I regretted my short stay at Washington. Congress interested me very much, and I could have wished to become better acquainted with its character and proceedings. Of the Senate I saw little. The delay in the election of a Speaker for the House of Representatives retarded the public business, and many of the leading senators had not arrived. Twice or thrice when I went to the Senate Chamber, the galleries were cleared in a short time, as the senators were

about to enter on an *executive session,* from
which strangers are excluded. Congress and
the Falls of Niagara were the greatest sights I
saw in the States. The latter have often been
described. It is to be hoped that some one
with more time and better opportunities will visit
Washington during the sitting of Congress, and
give a full sketch of that great and most interesting assembly.

At Washington (December 1859) I attended
a curious lecture on the " Politics of the Times,"
by Mr. Prentice, editor of a paper at Louisville,
in Kentucky. It seemed to be a sort of lament
over the degeneracy of the age, and consisted
mainly of general abuse of everything and
everybody. It was delivered *vivâ voce,* without
any aid from notes, and in a singularly chaste
and classic style; witty and epigrammatic—
forcible and terse. He saw many signs of the
break-up of the Union, and deplored the
approaching downfall of " a government which
is the glory and admiration of the world."
That such is the character of their government
I found to be the first article in the political
creed of every American. He pointed out
three giant evils in the present political condition of the United States:—The want of an
adequate and systematic training to educate

the people in their political duties, and enlighten them in the true principles of political science; the absence of any feeling of allegiance towards the general government in the great body of the people; and the non-existence of a patriotic feeling of nationality. Among the causes of these evils he adduced the degeneracy of public men; spoke of the talents, high standing, and statesmanship of Webster, Clay, Jackson, and Calhoun, and complained that there was now no one to replace them; said that the public men of the present day were, three-fourths of them, restless, turbulent, place-seeking, unscrupulous demagogues, and the remainder " dainty ama- 'teurs" without moral courage. The former pandered to every popular whim or passion to gain their object; the latter gave them a faint, timid opposition. Another cause was the extraordinary material prosperity of the country, which raised numbers of an inferior class suddenly to wealth and social position, and invested mere riches with undue influence. He did not enter into the subject of any definite remedies for these evils. Mr. Prentice was evidently a discontented man. His discourse was marked by great ability, and, as an intellectual effort, was well worth listening to. For any political purpose, it seemed to want definiteness and practical application, though he undoubtedly presented some general views of great interest.

The complaint made by Mr. Prentice, of the degeneracy of public men in America, is one which we meet repeatedly in the American papers. It is now attracting the serious attention of the most intelligent and patriotic minds in the United States; and it appears to me well worth while for us to know what the American press says on this all-important subject. The subjoined extracts are from United States papers of high standing: —

"Citizens of far-sighted sagacity — true statesmen—have gradually secluded themselves from public notice within the last quarter of a century, and small, petty, plundering interests have invested with power politicians of corresponding calibre, who have usurped place for the benefit of cliques and parties instead of the general good of the nation. The source of all our woes is, that while the country enjoys an unparalleled degree of prosperity, and never presented to the world so bright an example of greatness, its leading men are unworthy of its fame, and unfitted to control its destinies. Fifty years ago individuals did not dare to aspire to positions of confidence in the gift of the people, excepting upon some real or affected basis of experience, sagacity, and worth. Popular representatives in all stations, from the President down to the village constable, were selected with a view to their fitness to exercise their respective functions, and to shield their constituents from the troubles which are inseparable from the mutations of time, the instability of men's minds, and the fallibility of human institutions. Political storms were little feared, because the ship of State was known to be staunch and strong, and to be guided by skilful pilots. Within a quarter of a century this happy state of things has slowly but surely changed. Party lines have been gradually drawn away from national to individual concerns, and the elective franchise has been prostituted to fill public offices with tricksters and managers, so that place has become the invariable prey of the most venal jobber or cunning and successful intriguer. Not only in our large cities and upon our lines of communication, but in the National and State capitals, moneyed interests have successively outbidden each other for power, until the very existence of great men and pure minds has become frayed out of political life. The nomination and election of Mr. Lincoln to the Presidency of the United

States, are the last and most striking proofs of the truth of this assertion. Without any reference to personal merits or demerits, no individual so obscure could, in more halcyon days, or in a healthy state of the Confederation, have been bought forward for an office so responsible as the Chief Magistracy of thirty millions of people."

"Popular governments — that is, governments resting upon a broad suffrage basis and a free press—cannot permanently retain in their service the best men of the country. As the stream will not rise higher than its fountain, so a representative government, in the proper acceptation of that term, will only attract to its service the average talent and morality of the people represented. We have been feeling for years the silent operation of this law upon every department of our government, state and national. Every one who has made the effort knows how hard a thing it is to get our more worthy and capable citizens to accept political trusts of any description. To find America's great men we must seek the shades of professional life, or the great centres of material industry. We take little risk in saying that there are more of the higher qualities of manhood employed in directing the productive industry of this country than in all the executive departments of the federal government combined. Of course we must not be understood to intimate that first-class men are never to be found in political life among us, for the very statesman who has awakened these reflections would be a living and conclusive testimony against us. It cannot be disguised that many of the cleverest men this country has produced have devoted the best energies of their lives to political employments. So we often see men in other professions who waste a large portion of their abilities from never discovering, until it is too late, that they were out of place. We only speak of the tendency of our institutions to attract the average virtue and intelligence into the public service; and when they do attract a higher grade of men, it is, as a general thing, their misfortune; it conduces neither to their happiness nor to their usefulness, and, in nine cases out of ten, discharges them from its service disappointed, if not broken-hearted."—

"They traced this degradation and danger through the ramifications of trade, fashion, professional life, and manners, and almost demonstrated the essential truth of Macaulay's statements in regard to the effect of universal suffrage on this continent. There was nothing morbid, spiteful, or croaking in these views; they were illustrated by facts, proved by statistics, and the inference was irresistible that the cure of these prolific evils—the stay for this downward tendency—must be sought in *social* reformation; that individuals and communities must take a stand, apart from old party organizations, on the same principle that volunteer corps are raised during an invasion. There must be a propaganda, a fraternity based on disinterested fealty and reform—acting, writing, speaking in concert—until power is transferred once more to honest men, to intelligent citizens, and to patriots. In great exigencies such social combinations and protests have been effective—as witness the overthrow of the slave-trade, the temperance reformation, etc.; and the facts of the hour, and prospects of the future, warn us that the time approaches when, unless the good men and true, the wise and patriotic, join hands, and minds, and hearts, in this holy cause, what is now a vague and clemental, will become an organized and integral malady, fatal to the grandest experiment in self-government the world has ever seen!"

CHAPTER III.

THE SLAVERY QUESTION AND THE WAR OF RACES.

"There is a poor, blind Samson in this land,
   Shorn of his strength, and bound in bonds of steel,
Who may, in some grim revel, raise his hand,
   And shake the pillars of this Commonweal,
Till the vast temple of our liberties
A shapeless mass of wreck and rubbish lies."
                                           LONGFELLOW.

THE New World by no means realizes the peace and harmony of a golden age. Everywhere on the continent of North America contests are raging, arising chiefly out of the antipathy of race to race, or the incompatibility of one race or nation with another. The Pale Face and the Red Indian, the Caucasian and the Negro, the Celt and the Saxon, the French and the English, the North and the South, are either at open war or in a state of chronic discontent with one another; and, as if the prejudices of race do not engender enough of bitterness and animosity, religious feuds add fuel to the fire, and the enmities of Catholic and Protestant contribute in no small degree to the prevalent discord and strife. Of these perplexing questions of race, the most difficult and most formidable is that of the negroes, of whom there are nearly four millions in a state of slavery, and many others scattered through the United States and the British Colonies. Though we speak of them indiscriminately as one race, there are many varieties of them, very different from each other in character, disposition, and physical features. The majority seem to be a very fine race of people, light-hearted, cheerful, tractable, and industrious, with countenances beaming with kindliness and good-humour. No one who has resided for a day or two at the Waverley Hotel, in Halifax, can forget the very pleasant, polite, and really gentlemanly coloured waiter there, apparently a negro of unmixed blood; and in Halifax (where there are many negroes), as well as in the United States, numbers of similar countenances are seen amongst the coloured races. But the negroes are by no means all of such mild, pleasant dispositions; there are others of a very different aspect indeed, different in form of head and features, as well as in character and expression of countenance, where the bold, vigorous, determined, ruthless savage is written plainly in the face and bearing; who strikes you at once to be entirely out of place as the humble, attentive waiter in a hotel, and more fitted to seize and sell into slavery his fellow negro in Africa, or to lead a bloody insurrection against the whites in America. In a hotel at Philadelphia I saw a tall, fine, " distinguished "-looking negro, the very personification of disdain in look, attitudes, movements; and many are seen in the States with the well-marked expression of the fierce, relentless savage. When one meets such countenances, one cannot help fearing that a terrible day awaits the slave-holders and their families. The small, contracted forehead, generally found in the negro race, appears to indicate but moderate intelligence; and though some have evinced considerable mental capacity, such instances are rare, and there can be little doubt of the great natural inferiority of the negro to the white race. This seems the general conviction of the most intelligent of those friends of the negro in North America who have had the best opportunities of judging of his powers. Up to the age of about eleven or twelve years they are as capable of education as the whites, and able to stand their ground with them; but above that age, it is said, a marked difference appears; the negro comes to a stand, the white advances and leaves him behind.

The poor negro is in a truly unhappy condition in North America; there is no resting-place for him on that continent. He is a continual difficulty, to himself and to all classes of the whites—even to those who assume to be his friends. Though no doubt kindly treated and contented in many families in the South, he has no security for that happiness; is rigorously held to bondage, frequently cruelly used, and everywhere in the Southern States exposed to the action of very harsh laws, greatly aggravated in severity since the Northern abolition movement. If he ever obtains freedom in the South, there is too much reason to fear it will only be by fighting for it, as the slave-holders have committed themselves to extreme doctrines on the subject of slavery, and seem to be as fanatical on their side as the wild abolition party on the opposite side of the question. They now hold that the blacks are a race so far inferior as to be incapable of maintaining their position in competition with the whites; that they are fit only for slavery, and happier in that condition than they ever have been in freedom; and that the tropical soils cannot be cultivated except by the coloured races, who, they say, will labour only when compelled. The great convenience of such doctrines, the constant repetition of them, and the support they have received from other influential quarters, disinterested and intelligent, seem to have at last impressed the slave-owners with a thorough belief in them, as great fundamental principles firmly established. In a debate in the Senate, about the beginning of 1860, Mr. Brown, of Mississippi, said, "I declare again, what I did on a former occasion, that in my opinion slavery is a great moral, social, and political blessing— a blessing to the slave and a blessing to the master. As an evidence that it is no hardship to the negro, I repeat the assertion that four millions of the negro race in this Union are to-day in better circumstances, morally, socially, and religiously, than four millions of the same race anywhere upon the habitable globe. I submit that proposition to the Senate; and if there be four millions of the negro race so happy, well contented, well provided for, so moral, religious, and occupying so high a social position, tell me where they are to be found? If they are nowhere to be found, then how can you assume that they have been debased by their servile condition? How will you prove that slavery has degraded them if they are better off here than anywhere else? Slavery is the normal condition of the negro, whether we look at him as a moral, social, or religious, or simply as a physical being. In every possible aspect he is more prosperous in slavery than in any other condition. Mr. Brown also replied to the remark of Mr. Trumbull, that slavery was a wrong to the negro because it violated his inalienable rights as a man, by saying that the senator himself admitted that all laws were, to a greater or less degree, an infringement on these inalienable rights. The only question, then, was whether any political community were not best qualified to judge, in its own peculiar condition, how much restraint shall be imposed upon the various classes of its members."

The same senator, in an address to his constituents, said—" I want Cuba, I want Tamaulipas, Potosi, and one or two other Mexican states, and I want them all for the same reason, for the planting and spreading of slavery. And a footing in Central America will powerfully aid us in acquiring those other states. Yes, I want these countries for the spread of slavery. I would spread the blessings of slavery like the religion of our Divine Master, to the uttermost ends of the earth; and, rebellious and wicked as the Yankees have been, I would even extend it to them."

In the House of Representatives, Mr. Anderson of Missouri, stated—" We honestly and conscientiously believe, that the fittest condition for the negro race is that of slavery. We believe that the master is necessary to the support, comfort, and happiness of the slave, and that the negro race is unfitted for the enjoyment of civil liberty."

There can be little doubt that a large proportion of the slave-owners are perfectly sincere in the opinion that slavery is advantageous to the negro, and that it is the condition for which he is best fitted. They have imbibed that doctrine from their earliest years, their interests are identified with it; they hear it from their own ministers of religion, and from some of the most distinguished of the clergymen of the Free States of the North; the ethnologists of America tell them so; and they are further strengthened in their convictions by the support of many of the highest minds in all parts of the Union, by the weak and shallow character of the writings of many of the abolitionists; by the manifest repulsion the whites of the North exhibit towards the negro, and by his miserable condition in freedom in Canada and the Northern States.

They would be more than mortal if they could resist all these influences.

A leading New York paper says :—" So far from believing negro slavery a curse, we regard it as a great blessing in the tropical climates, and in the Southern States of our republic—a blessing to the slave, to the master, and to the whole of this Union—one of the great sources of our national prosperity." Recently a number of sermons have been delivered in the city of New York, touching more or less on the subject of slavery. In numbers of these, slavery has been held not to be condemned by Scripture. Among those who insisted on this, were three very distinguished clergymen, in that great free city—the Rev. Henry J. Van Dyke, of the first Presbyterian Church, Brooklyn; the Rev. Dr. Francis Vinton, of Trinity Church (Episcopalian), Broadway; and the Rev. Dr. Raphael, Rabbi of the Jewish Synagogue. In Nova Scotia, I met with many who had visited both the Southern States and the West Indies; and of these I found scarcely one who sided with the Northern abolition party, some who in part coincided with Southern opinions, and many, who, deploring the existence of slavery and admitting its evils, doubted the success of a policy of emancipation, saw no prospect of freedom for the slaves without some fearful convulsion, and confessed frankly that it was a difficulty of a most perplexing character, and they did not see their way to get rid of it.

Thus confirmed in their ideas, and scorning to yield, the planters, whose courage and spirit one cannot but admire, believe that they can hold their own, and will take no steps for that gradual emancipation which many of their best friends think the only security for themselves, and the only method of bringing about, peacefully and safely, that freedom for the slaves, which, sooner or later, must come—probably all the sooner if the slave States secede, and lose the benefit of Northern protection.

But slavery is not the only discouraging feature in the prospects of the negro race in America; there is, besides, the rooted antipathy entertained towards them by the whites. Slavery may, and probably will, be abolished some day. This repulsion cannot be done away with. It is manifested in a thousand ways in the free States and in the British Colonies. There the blacks are despised and shunned—treated as an inferior race—thereby mortified and degraded, and deprived of many opportunities of evincing their capacities and improving their condition. In the cities in the northern United States separate omnibuses are provided for "coloured persons." If, by any chance, a negro boy gets admission to a school beside white children (in British America; this could not be in the United States), the latter move off from him as if he had some infectious disease, and sit apart. In Halifax lately there was a striking display of this feeling. A negro volunteer corps had been formed; the other companies would not allow them to come near them, to mingle with them, in event of any united movements rendering it desirable to equalise the companies—they must be kept at a distance. They are not admitted into the militia or upon juries in Massachusetts. In Canada, lately, an English female missionary, who married a coloured preacher, was mobbed and insulted by, it is said, *respectable citizens*, and sent to Coventry by the people of the place. Recently the city of New York, by an overwhelming majority, has rejected the proposal to extend somewhat the right of suffrage enjoyed by the coloured race (at present limited to those who possess freeholds of £50 in value); and a leading paper of that metropolitan city declares, "The African race cannot be admitted to an equal social and political status with the superior white race." The new President of the

United States, Mr. Lincoln, the choice of the Republican party, said, in 1858, in a speech on the all-absorbing question :—" Make them politically and socially our equals? My own feelings will not admit of this; and, if mine would, we know that those of the great mass of white people will not. Whether this feeling accords with justice and sound judgment is not the sole question, if, indeed, it is any part of it. A universal feeling, whether well or ill founded, cannot be disregarded. We cannot, then, make them equals." With such prejudices against them, even among those most friendly towards them, and having to compete with a clever, well-educated, and most energetic people, the coloured races are depressed and confined to the lowest and poorest occupations. They have no chance in North America of proving their fitness for freedom. Indeed, one of the free States last admitted into the Union, Oregon, refuses the right of voting to "negroes, Chinamen, and mulattoes;" and in a clause, carried by a majority of 8,640 to 1,081 votes, denies free negroes, in future, admission to the State. "No free negro or mulatto, not residing in this State at the time of the adoption of this constitution, shall come, reside, or be within this State, or hold any real estate, or make any contracts, or maintain any suit therein; and the legislative assembly shall provide, by penal laws, for the removal, by public officers, of all such negroes and mulattoes, and for their effectual exclusion from this State, and for the punishment of persons who shall bring them into the State, or employ or harbour them therein."

In Illinois, also a free State, negroes are not now admitted to reside. Those already there are not allowed to vote, to serve on juries, or to marry white women. Mr. Lamar, of Mississippi, in one of the never-ending debates on slavery, retorted upon a Republican as follows:—" It was stated that the object of the revolutionary war was to establish an absolute equality of rights, socially and politically. The gentleman from Connecticut who asserted this ought to have had the candour to hold up his own State to reprehension for violating these principles of equality; for in Connecticut the negro is neither politically nor socially equal with the white man; but, on the contrary, he is deprived of the right of voting; he is held incompetent to be a witness; he is precluded from the privilege of intermarrying with whites; and the people guard, sedulously, against all contact between them" It has been made abundantly plain that the statement in the Declaration of

Independence, that all men are created equal, and the consequences deduced from it, were intended to be applied to the white race only. The Republican party desires to get rid of them, and several of their leaders have mooted a scheme for sending them to some of the tropical regions of America. Mr. Wade, a Republican senator from Ohio, lately expressed himself as follows regarding them :—

" There was another project for which he hoped not only the Republican party but philanthropists of all parties would unite. The free negroes in this country were despised by all, repudiated by all, and outcasts upon the face of the earth. They were the victims of a deep-rooted prejudice. He would not argue whether that prejudice was right or wrong, for he knew that it was immoveable. These two races could not occupy the same neighbourhood and both be prosperous and happy. He therefore hoped means would be provided, whereby this class of unfortunate men might emigrate to some congenial climate, where their mental, moral, and physical natures might find development, and where the white man degenerates in the same proportion that the black man prospers. Let them go to the tropics. He understood that arrangements might be made with some of the

Central American States for this purpose. He hoped to hear no more about negro equality at the North, for there was no more desire to have this class at the North than at the South. Let them go to some place where they can rise in the scale of being to their fullest development, and enjoy all the rights and blessings of which man is capable."

Amongst other causes of dislike, the whites apprehend the amalgamation of races which may take place, and the result of which they are convinced, is to degrade the posterity, and make them sink towards the level of the inferior race. They fear the deterioration of their own race, and desire to get rid of the coloured races altogether; a great negro exodus to some tropical region of America, is at present a favourite scheme, though how it is to be brought about, and the safety of such a negro nation, if it could be brought about, in contact with filibustering whites, are very far from being clear. Such is the unhappy position of the negro race in North America. All shun them and desire to get rid of them, excepting those who make slaves of them.

Slavery, which there now seems reason to fear will cause the break-up of the great American Republic, has been a most embarrassing question from the beginning. Its present position will be better understood by a glance at its previous history.

Slavery and the slave-trade are inheritances which the people of the United States derived from their ancestors, the British colonists. Up to a late period, both were sanctioned by the British people and Government. The British slave-trade, which had enriched the merchants of Liverpool and Bristol, was suppressed in the year 1807; and slavery in the British dominions was abolished in the years 1833-38; the West India planters receiving from Parliament twenty millions sterling in compensation. Some of the colonies had, at times, protested against the slave-trade, but their objections were overruled by the British authorities. At a meeting in Virginia, in 1774, at which Washington presided, the persons present declared their "most earnest wishes to see a stop put for ever to such a wicked, cruel, and unnatural trade." Towards the close of the struggle for independence, the state of Massachusetts put an end to slavery within her limits. Pennsylvania (1780) and other Northern States (1784) forbade the importation of slaves, and declared that thereafter all born upon their soil should be free. Soon there grew up a broad line of distinction between free and slave States, or North and

South, which has increased and become more marked up to the present time. Virginia, Maryland, and North Carolina prohibited or discouraged the importation of slaves (1778-86), in which they were soon followed by New York and New Jersey. Slavery did not cease entirely in the latter States till 1830, or later.

The greatest of the statesmen who were members of the Convention which formed the Constitution in the year 1787, as Washington, Jefferson, Franklin, Hamilton, were strongly averse to perpetuating the system of slavery. But, it must be particularly noticed, that they were unable to embody their views in the Magna Charta of America. That great basis of the Union most distinctly recognized and protected slavery; unless this had been done the Union could never have been formed. And, up to the present day, slavery has been equally recognized and protected by the two authorized interpreters of the Constitution, Congress and the Supreme Court of the United States.

1. The Constitution authorized the continuance of the slave-trade for twenty years—till 1808. This traffic had been condemned by the Continental Congress of 1774, but, in 1787, for the purpose of securing the adhesion of South Carolina and Georgia, it was sanctioned

till 1808. In reference to this and other provisions encouraging slavery, some member said that such features in the Constitution were " inconsistent with the principles of the Revolution, and dishonourable to the American character." To this it was replied, " Let every State import what it pleases. The morality or wisdom of slavery is a consideration belonging to the States."—" Religion and humanity had nothing to do with this question. Interest alone is the governing principle with nations." —" The true question at present is, whether the Southern States shall or shall not be parties to this Union." To this threat of withdrawing from the Union, the Northern members succumbed, and, being conciliated by some favourable commercial regulations, they conceded what the slave States required of them. The clauses in the national charter bearing upon slavery, and the subsequent enactments of Congress upon the subject, have been, as on this point, a long series of compromises.

2. While the slaves were not allowed votes, three-fifths of their number were to be reckoned as part of the population entitled to members in the House of Representatives, by which a considerable legislative power was thrown into the hands of the whites in the slave States.

3. A Fugitive Slave Law was also specially enforced in the Constitution.

The following are the clauses in the Constitution bearing directly or indirectly on the slavery question:

"*A*. Representatives and direct taxes shall be apportioned among the several States which may be included within this Union, according to their respective numbers, which shall be determined by adding to the whole number of free persons, including those bound to service for a term of years, and excluding Indians not taxed, three-fifths of all other persons.

"*B*. The migration or importation of such persons as any of the States now existing shall think proper to admit, shall not be prohibited by the Congress prior to the year one thousand eight hundred and eight; but a tax or duty may be imposed on such importation, not exceeding ten dollars for each person.

"*C*. The citizens of each State shall be entitled to all privileges and immunities of citizens in the several States.

"*D*. No person held to service or labour in one State, under the laws thereof, escaping into another, shall, in consequence of any law or regulation therein, be discharged from such service or labour, but shall be delivered up on the claim of the party to whom such service or labour may be due.

"E. The Congress shall have power to dispose of, and make all needful rules and regulations respecting the territory or other property belonging to the United States.

"F. The United States shall guarantee to every State in this Union, a Republican form of Government, and shall protect each of them against invasion; and, on application of the Legislature, or of the Executive (when the Legislature cannot be convened), against domestic violence.

"G. The powers not delegated to the United States by the Constitution, nor prohibited by it to the States, are reserved to the States respectively, or to the people.

"H. Congress shall have power to exercise exclusive legislation in all cases whatsoever, over such district (not exceeding ten miles square) as may, by cession of particular States, and the acceptance of Congress, become the seat of the Government of the United States, and to exercise like authority over all places purchased by the consent of the legislature of the State in which the same shall be, for the erection of forts, magazines, arsenals, dockyards, and other needful buildings."

It is sometimes supposed that Congress took up a decided position against the extension of slavery by the ordinance of 1787, which prohibited slavery in the north-west territory, between the Ohio and Mississippi rivers. It is true, that at the time, under the influence of Jefferson, such was the disposition of Congress, mainly because such was the wish of those who ceded these lands. But two years after, even under the presidency of Washington, Congress agreed to a quite different arrangement; for then, the Union accepted the western lands of North Carolina, surrendered on the express condition "that no regulation made, or to be made by Congress, should tend to the emancipation of slaves;" and in 1802, Georgia made the same stipulation when she ceded her western territory to Congress. It must not be supposed that Congress forced the prohibition of slavery on those who ceded the north-western territory; she simply received the territory on such conditions as were acceptable to those who gave it. From time to time new States were formed out of these various territories, and admitted to join the Union, some as free States, some as slave States.

Neither the Constitution nor the Acts of Congress exhibit any fundamental principle or any definite line of action regarding this troubled question; now one side has had the advantage, now the other, according to the circumstances of the case. Upon surveying the whole course of Congress, it would appear that the desires of the people of the region which was the subject of dispute have generally been complied with, though this was not explicitly put forward as a guiding principle till the passage of Mr. Douglas' Kansas-Nebraska Act, in 1854, which established what is called *Popular Sovereignty* for the territories; that is, that a new State should be slave or free according as its inhabitants should desire. The only decided action previously taken by Congress on the subject of slavery was shortly after the formation of the Constitution, abjuring all right of interference with the States on the subject. In consequence of petitions against slavery, it was ordered to be entered on the journals, " That Congress have no authority to interfere in the emancipation of slaves, or in the treatment of them in any of the States; it remaining with the several States alone to provide any regulations therein which humanity and true policy may require."

As it was thus settled that each State is absolute sovereign as to its own internal regulations, and that neither Congress nor any one State has the right to interfere with slavery in any of the States, it might have been supposed that no agitation on the subject could arise to disturb the peace of the Union. But four questions connected with slavery have sprung up—the Fugitive Slave Law, slavery in the District of Columbia, slavery in the territories, and the demand for abolition raised in some of the Northern States.

Slaves frequently escape from the slave into the free States. By the Constitution the owners have the right to follow them there, and take them back. The great majority of the people of the free States sympathize with the poor negro endeavouring to escape from bondage, aid him in every way in their power, and by secret arrangements, known as *the underground railway*, forward him to Canada, where he is safe from pursuit. Even the authorities in the free States lend unwilling aid to the slave-owner in this slave-hunt; and at times the people have been so excited that the runaway could not be secured without the aid of the military. Further, several of the Northern States have, by their legislatures, passed *Personal Liberty* Acts, calculated (though ostensibly for defence of their own citizens) to impede or prevent the capture of fugitive slaves; acts at variance with the constitutional compact between them and the slave States, as well as with various deliberate acts of Congress. The Southerners are enraged at this resistance to the recovery of *their property* and defiance of the provisions of the Constitution and the law in their favour; while the Northerners loathe the odious task assigned to them of depriving a fellow-creature of his liberty for no crime. A constant and increasing irritation is kept up, and North and South become more and more alienated from each other. DANIEL WEBSTER, one of the most distinguished statesmen and orators of the North, in a great measure lost his popularity and influence there because, in 1850, he lent his powerful aid in passing a bill for rendering the Fugitive Slave Law more efficient. However averse to the whole system of slavery, it was his opinion, as a lawyer and a statesman, that the slave States had a right to this protection. This is one of the most difficult to be adjusted of the points at issue between the North and the South. The system of slavery cannot be maintained in the Union without some such law, and the free States of the North and North-west cannot be reconciled to the part they are required to take in enforcing it.

The DISTRICT OF COLUMBIA is a small portion of the State of Maryland, on the left bank of the river Potomac, which is the seat of the Government of the United States, and under the direct control of Congress. Its extent is sixty-three square miles, and its population, in 1850, was 51,687, of whom 40,000 were in the city of Washington. Of the 51,687, 38,027 are whites, 9973 free coloured persons, and 3687 are slaves. The Anti-slavery party, assuming, as they always do, that freedom is the national *rule*, and slavery only an *exception*, allowed in certain States by special compact, demand that Congress should enforce the rule and free the slaves in this district, over which it has exclusive control; while the opposite party maintain that the perfect neutrality of Congress is its proper ground on the slavery question, and oppose any interference of Congress with the existing state of things; and at the same time they naturally object to freeing the negroes in the District of Columbia, imbedded between the slave States of Virginia and Maryland.

The irritation between the North and the South on the subject of slavery is also kept up by the violent proceedings and harangues of the Northern abolitionists, ardent lovers of liberty, who desire to extend to the negro the same freedom which they themselves enjoy, and to blot out what they consider as a dark stain on the great Republic. While thus acknowledging some good motives as prompting them, it cannot be denied that they have been rash and indiscreet in their officious intermeddling with a delicate question, which numbers of them seemed incapable of understanding; that their conduct has been harsh, irritating, and offensive towards the South; that in their schemes they have been reckless of every consideration of good faith or justice, and have done much to endanger the lives of their Southern fellow-citizens, and to disturb the peace of the Union. But they will be best described by the words of the celebrated Dr. Channing, well known as no friend or apologist of slavery:—

"The Abolitionists have done wrong, I believe; nor is their wrong to be winked at because done fanatically or with good intentions, for how much mischief may be wrought with good designs! They have fallen into the common error of enthusiasts, that of exaggerating their object—of feeling as if no evil existed but that which they opposed, and as if no guilt could be compared with that of countenancing and upholding it. The tone of their newspapers, so far as I have seen them, has often been fierce, bitter, and abusive. They have sent forth their orators, some of them transported with fiery zeal, to sound the alarm against slavery through the land, to gather together young and old, pupils from schools, females hardly arrived at years of discretion, the ignorant, the excitable, the impetuous, and to organize these into associations for the battle against oppression. Very unhappily, they preached their doctrine to the coloured people, and collected them into societies. To this mixed and excitable multitude, minute heart-rending descriptions of slavery were given in piercing tones of passion, and slaveholders were held up as monsters of cruelty and crime. The Abolitionist, indeed, proposed to convert slaveholders; and for this end he approached them with vituperation, and exhausted on them the vocabulary of his abuse. And he has reaped as he sowed."

In the years 1832-6, there was extreme excitement in the United States on the slavery question. Abolitionism was rampant in the North, in great meetings, associations, speeches, pamphlets, newspapers. It demanded that the slave should be freed, without consideration for the Constitution, the rights of the States, the claims of the master, or the prospects of the slave. Its violence produced a reaction against it, even in the North itself. In the South, post-offices were broken into, and anti-slavery papers, which were thought calculated to excite disaffection and insurrection, were seized and destroyed; while a Southern movement in favour of freeing the slave was arrested, disunion and non-intercourse with the North were talked of, a bitterness of feeling was created which has never abated, and harsher measures were adopted towards both the coloured race and their Southern advocates. Congress refused to receive memorials on the subject of slavery. In 1859 Abolitionism culminated in the Harper's Ferry Insurrection in Virginia, when John Brown, a man who, it is said, had had some hard usage in Kansas, and who, it is also alleged, had perpetrated some very dark deeds there, with sixteen white men and five negroes, took forcible possession of the United States armoury at Harper's Ferry, killed four of the inhabitants, and seized others, who were detained as prisoners. His intention was understood to be to raise the slaves into insurrection and establish a revolutionary government. But the slaves did not join him, and he and his adherents were overpowered, brought to trial, and executed. The Southern States were greatly irritated by this; and still more by the sympathy openly shown for Brown and his associates in the Northern States.—The Abolition party in the United States has been in no small degree encouraged in its reckless course by certain sympathizers in this country. But they have not gone to the most judicious quarters for advice. There are no more zealous or more able friends of emancipation than Lord Brougham and the "Westminster Review;" and it might have been better for America had this party been animated by the temperate spirit which characterized his Lordship's late letter to some ardent Boston Abolitionists, and the article on the slavery question in the last number of that celebrated journal.

But the greatest of the questions at issue between the North and the South are those relating to the territories: Shall slavery be permitted in them? shall the new States to be formed from them be slave or free States? Each State elects two members to the Senate, from which each party desires to get possession of the new States, merely as sources of direct political power. The Southerners, especially the non-slaveholding whites, who are, also, ambitious to have slaves, desire to see new fields opened for slave-labour; and the Northern slave States may be regarded greatly as slave-growing States, and look for new markets for their peculiar produce. On the other hand, the great Free-soil party of the North and West, also seeking outlets for their population and their enterprise, desire that the new States shall be free from so pernicious an institution as slavery. The Constitution is not definite in its language bearing on such questions; each party interprets it according to its own principles, and hence the interminable and perplexed disputes as to slavery in the territories.

Up to the year 1819, the parties were exactly equal as to the new States received into the Union. Four free States had been admitted—Vermont, formed from part of the territory of New York; and Ohio, Indiana, and Illinois, parts of the North-west territory ceded to the Union in 1787. Four slave States had been admitted—Kentucky, formed from the territory of Virginia; Tenessee, from the territory ceded by North Carolina; Louisiana, acquired from France in 1803; and Mississippi, from South Carolina.

In 1819 another slave State, Alabama, part of the lands ceded by Georgia and South Carolina, entered the Union; and, about the same time, Missouri, a slave-holding territory, part of the tract called Louisiana, west of the Mississippi, acquired from France, was proposed, making a sixth slave State, while only four free States had joined the Union. The Anti-slavery party took alarm, and a memorable contest ensued, which agitated the whole country for upwards of two years. This party made earnest opposition to the demand of Missouri for admission, desiring to prevent the further spread of the system of slavery, which appeared to be not only becoming permanently fixed, but increasing; and as a party, they resisted a measure which would increase the slave power in the Senate. They urged that slavery should not be permitted in any State or territory where it could be prohibited, holding that Congress had power over the territories, and that the prohibition of slavery in the North-west territory in 1787, evinced the desire of Congress to prevent the extension of slavery wherever it could. They also represented that it was now the turn for the admission of a free State; the last admitted, Alabama, being a slave State. The other party said that forcing Missouri to become a free State, would be a violation of the Constitution, which leaves each State free to settle for itself the question of slavery and all other matters not expressly assigned to the Federal Government—that the voice of the people was the guiding authority in all points not settled by the Constitution; and that, as the people of Missouri wished to keep slaves, it would be arbitrary and despotic to coerce them into the opposite system. These arguments had great weight, from the acknowledged system of independence and sovereignty of the individual States, and the supremacy of the popular will—both fundamental principles of the American system. It was urged in opposition that Missouri was under the rule of Congress as a territory (see clause E, page 173), and that she was not one of the original thirteen between whom the compact of the Constitution was made, and the inference was thence drawn that Congress had the right to regulate the terms of her admission. But the feeling prevailed that the new States should have the same privileges of sovereignty in their internal affairs as the original States assumed on forming the contract of union. The will of the people then, as now, had great force; and, as Missouri desired slavery, and as the Pro-slavery party was predominant in Congress, she was admitted as a slave State in the year 1821. At the same time, Maine, north of Massachusetts, was admitted as a free State, and the opponents of slavery were enabled to procure an enactment prohibiting slavery in the territory north of the parallel of latitude 36 deg. 30 min. north, except in the part of Missouri north of that line —the question being left open as to territory south of that line. This was termed *The Missouri Compromise*, now quite famous in the history of the United States.

This Compromise allayed the storm arising out of the territorial question for nearly thirty years. Up to the year 1850 six new States joined the Union; three Free—Michigan, Wisconsin, and Iowa; and three Slave States— Arkansas, Florida, and Texas. There was great opposition to the admission of Texas, partly on account of the very questionable manner in which the annexation of that republic was brought about; partly because being of very large size, it was to form four States when the population was sufficient, and would thus greatly increase the political influence of the Proslavery party. Slavery was to be prohibited in new States formed out of that part of the State north of 36 deg. 30 min. north latitude. States formed out of Texas south of that line (much the greater portion) were to be "admitted into the Union with or without slavery, as the people of each State asking admission may desire." Texas still remains a single State.

The immense accession of territory at the close of the war with Mexico, in 1848, again brought up the question as to slavery in territories or new States. A large portion of the new tracts of country, including about half of California and the greater part of New Mexico, was *south* of the Compromise line of 36 deg. 30 min., and the Pro-slavery party thought it should be their own. It is true that by the terms of the Act the Compromise line applied only to the territory immediately west of the river Mississippi, ceded by France to the United States, under the name of Louisiana; but the upholders of slavery considered that it should extend also through the newly-acquired territory to the Pacific. But California, which had increased greatly in population in consequence of its rich gold mines, and very much by emigration from the free States of the Union, in 1849 applied for admission as a free State; and the people of New Mexico were at that time supposed to tend in the same direction. The slave State, Texas, had also some claim on the territory of New Mexico. Parties were greatly excited. Senators from the South declared that the prohibition of slavery in these regions would lead to a break-up of the Union. Again and again it was moved to cut off from the proposed new State of California all that lay south of the parallel 36 deg. 30 min. north latitude, that southern part to be a territory to be admitted as a State at a future time, with or without slavery, as the people might then desire; but without success. At length a compromise, supported by the distinguished leaders, Clay, of the South; and Webster, of the North, was agreed on. California, in her full extent, was admitted as a free State. Utah, mostly north of 36 deg. 30 min., and New Mexico, mostly south of that line, were formed into Territories, without any restriction as to slavery, that being reserved for future adjustment. Texas, for an indemnity of about £2,000,000 sterling, gave up its claim on New Mexico; the slave-trade was prohibited in the district of Columbia; and a more efficient measure was passed for the recovery of fugitive slaves. This was the *Compromise of* 1850.

Though not settled till the year 1850, the agitation as to the territory obtained by conquest from Mexico had been going on, more or less, for four years. Shortly after the war commenced, in 1846, Congress, with prudent foresight, placed a large sum at the disposal of

the President, to enable him to compensate
Mexico for any territory to be acquired on the
conclusion of a peace. A Mr. Wilmot moved
in the House of Representatives, that slavery
be prohibited in the territory to be acquired
from Mexico. This, usually known as the
Wilmot Proviso, passed the House of Representatives, but was lost in the Senate. Thus, the
Congress of the United States was actually
occupied in making arrangements for the
government of a territory nearly two years
before it ceased to belong to another power!
Who can deny that Brother Jonathan goes
a-head?

The important question of slavery in the
Territories soon assumed a new phase, towards
which it had undoubtedly been tending for some
time, but which was not fully developed till the
passage of the Kansas-Nebraska Act in 1854.
In this new aspect it became more intricate,
involved in legal subtleties, and various difficulties as to the true interpretation of the Constitution, and the powers of Congress.

At the time of the formation of the Constitution (1787), the slave-holding party was
undoubtedly somewhat depressed. The slave-trade was to be abolished after twenty years, and
some imagined that with its abolition slavery

would soon die out; the great North-west territory, by a solemn ordinance of Congress in the same year, was consecrated to freedom; seven of the thirteen States were, or soon were to be, free States; and the opinions of the great men who were mainly instrumental in forming the Constitution of the Union and bringing it into successful operation, were known to be unfavourable to slavery. These circumstances encouraged the Anti-slavery party to take for granted assumptions upon which they have constantly acted, that the free system of the Northern States was to be regarded as the system countenanced by the Union; that the existence of slavery in any State was an unfortunate, but unavoidable exception; that the institution was tolerated there only by special contract, and was everywhere else to be discouraged and prevented from spreading. But this view has never been admitted by the other party, who hold that strict neutrality on the question is enjoined by the Constitution. In short, the Republican party hold that slavery is *unlawful* everywhere, except where a sovereign *State* makes a special enactment sanctioning it. The Democratic party hold that slavery is *lawful* everywhere, except where such a sovereign State has by special enactment forbid it.

The slave States formed no less than six of
the original thirteen States, embracing a vast
territory, considerably larger than that of the
seven free States; up to 1850 they kept pace
with the latter in the admission of new States,
nine of each party having joined the Union
from the entrance of Vermont, in 1793, to that
of California in 1850. The soil of the slave
States is rich and fertile, and by its productive-
ness has contributed materially to the wealth
and prosperity of the Union. Till lately, they
have had the control of the Legislature and the
Government, and hitherto, a very large proportion (I think, the greater proportion) of the
men of statesman-like talent has come from the
South, or been united to the party of the South.
They have been all along too numerous a party,
too influential, too talented, to accept the inferior position which the other party endeavoured to assign to them, as the adherents of a
barbarous institution, tolerated only for a time,
and exceptionally.

The slave States had sufficient influence to
assert perfect equality with other States in the
Constitution which cemented the Union, and
in legislative enactments, and the admission of
new States, up to the year 1850, when California, a free State, was admitted. But the last

slave State, Texas, had joined in 1845, and there were no new slave States in prospect to enable upholders of slavery to maintain their power, while the North and West were rapidly filling up with the free-soil party, and would soon claim admission to the Union; in fact, Minesota in 1858, and Oregon in 1859, have been admitted as free States, and there is no slave State to balance them. Cuba, so long sought to strengthen the South, seems as distant as ever. They will be in a minority in the Senate, which is composed of two members from each State; they were in danger of being swamped in the House of Representatives by the rapid increase of population in the States of the North and North-west; while there was a fear that (what has actually taken place) a President opposed to them might be chosen, and thus the power of the Government thrown into their enemies' hands. Their power was on the wane, unless something could be done to stay the progress of the much-hated Black Republicans.

The Missouri Compromise seemed to shut them out from the North. They were still strong enough, however, to overturn that famous compact, and open out the wide regions of the North to settlers with slaves, who, if in sufficient numbers, would determine a new State in favour of slavery.

The Pro-slavery party in the United States has ever been rich in audacity and talent. When pressed hard by the doctrines of the Abolitionists, they boldly advanced to higher ground, and maintained that slavery is right, founded on justice, reason, and humanity, supported by Scripture, and in reality a beneficent institution, advantageous to the negro. In like manner, when power seemed about to fall from their hands by the increasing proportion of free States in the Union, and increase of population in the free States, they drew from the Constitution the doctrine of *Popular Sovereignty in the Territories*, and used it to overthrow the Missouri Compromise, and bring the whole of the Territories within their reach.

By the Constitution, Congress has the power to " dispose of, and make all needful rules and regulations for the Territory, or other property of the United States." This is the only clause which appears to authorize Congress to prohibit slavery in a territory. But the Pro-slavery party hold that, in reality, it conveys no such authority. They argue that it applies to territory only as land or property, not as a political community; that rules and regulations for territory as property, made by the temporary guardian of it, never could have meant a permanent system of legislation and government for its inhabitants; that such a supposition would make Congress a despot as regards the people of the Territories; be opposed to the whole spirit of the American Constitution, and particularly to that part which it guards so jealously, the sovereignty of each State as to its own internal concerns; that in all preceding cases, Congress, in granting admission to a State, had given it the Constitution acceptable to its inhabitants at the time of its entering the Union, and that it would be better to place the settlement of important questions directly in the hands of those most interested; that any sweeping exclusion or enforcement of slavery in the Territories would be prejudging a question which its inhabitants, the best judges, should alone have the power of determining; that the Territory was the common property of the whole Union, and that, therefore, every citizen, of whatever part of the Union, had the right to settle in it, with or without slaves, as he thought proper, so long as it remained the property of the whole, and was not, by admission as a State, assigned and set aside as the special possession of the politically organized inhabitants. It was further contended that the Compromise of 1850 had practically set aside the Missouri Compromise, the free State of California extending south of the line of 36 deg. 30 min.; while Utah, north of it, and New Mexico, were left to the pleasure of the settlers as to their domestic institutions.

The general views regarding the Territories just exhibited, were first presented publicly by the distinguished American statesman, General Cass, about the end of the year 1847, in a letter on the subject of the Wilmot Proviso; and on the principles of the American system, there seemed much force in the considerations which he brought forward on this difficult question. The principle of allowing the settlers themselves to determine whether their State should be slave or free, seemed to flow logically from the American system of the sovereignty of the individual States; it had a democratic look, and was so far successful for a time, that it was embodied in an act termed the Kansas-Nebraska Act in 1854, the Missouri Compromise being at the same time repealed, and slavery being allowed north of that line, if it could gain a footing there. Senator Douglas, from the free State of Illinois, was the chief promoter of this measure, which greatly irritated the Anti-slavery party, and may be said to have laid the foundation of the present powerful Republican party.

Not long after, the Supreme Court of the United States, in a celebrated decision in the case of Dred Scott, a negro who claimed his freedom from having resided with his master in the territory north of 36 deg. 30 min. north latitude, in which slavery was prohibited, pronounced the Missouri Compromise unconstitutional, beyond the power of Congress, and altogether of no avail or force in law; declared that "the Constitution recognizes the right of property of the master in a slave, and makes no distinction between that description of property and other property owned by a citizen;" that territory acquired, is acquired by the people of the United States, for their common and equal benefit, through their agent and trustee, the Federal Government; that Congress has no right to prohibit the citizens of any particular State or States from taking up their homes in such territory, nor from taking any description of their property there with them, including slaves, since the Constitution recognizes slaves as property; and that Congress has no power to exercise more authority over property of that description, than it may constitutionally exercise over property of any other kind; that the only function of Congress in regard to a Territory is to preserve it for the people to inhabit it, who, when in sufficient numbers, are to form a sovereign *State*, with whatever laws and institutions they please, not opposed to the Constitution of the United States.

It would be presumptuous to dispute the conformity of the strict letter of the Constitution with the interpretation of it thus given by the eminent lawyers who compose the Supreme Court of the United States; and their interpretation looks very logical and consistent indeed. But there are powers above law and constitutions, the powers of justice and humanity; circumstances arise which laws did not contemplate and failed to provide for; and the free States of the North considered themselves authorized and called upon by these higher powers, and by such circumstances, to do their utmost to check the spread of the dark spot on the national banner; they thought that an Act of Congress, emanating from some of the greatest statesmen of the nation, and in force upwards of thirty years, could not, in spirit, be very bad law; they judged that a co-partnery like the Union could not be without the power of excluding a proposed new partner distasteful to the majority, and they set to with vigour to get a majority in Congress and the Government based upon the great principle of preventing the further extension of slavery. There they are upon safe ground, whether resting on the Constitution or not, in a position in which they will command the sympathy and respect of the civilized world. They now have, or soon will have, the ascendancy, and (unless a new compromise is entered into) will use their power to exclude slavery from every new territory. They will do so by the right of the majority, and it will be a happy thing for the Union. At the same time, it must be admitted, that, as a *general and permanent* line of action, it will be new, neither required by the Constitution nor in unison with previous Acts of Congress; hence the secession of the slave States from the Union, which has entered on a new course of policy, injurious to their interests.

The passage of the Kansas-Nebraska Act in 1854 was followed by one of the most extraordinary struggles ever witnessed in a civilized country, and then by civil war. The scene of the contest was the territory of KANSAS, in the very centre of the United States, adjoining on the west the slave State Missouri, and just north of the compromise line of 36 deg. 30 min.

Missouri, having the free States of Illinois and Iowa on the east and north, feared to have another free State on its western border, by which it would be in a manner imbedded in freedom, a very bad position for slavery; and made every effort to plant settlers in Kansas, that when admitted as a State it might have a majority of its inhabitants in favour of slavery. The free States made similar exertions; and an "Emigrants' Aid Society," established in Massachusetts, gathered large funds, and in the year 1855 sent out numbers of emigrants to settle in Kansas. The Pro-slavery party appeared at first triumphant, and elected a legislative assembly in favour of their views. But the other party protested energetically against this body, and declared that its election was vitiated by the votes of members not resident in the State; that "large bodies of armed men from the State of Missouri appeared at the polls in most of the districts, and by most violent and tumultuous carriage and demeanour overawed the defenceless inhabitants, and by their own votes elected a large majority of the members of both Houses of the said Assembly." Accordingly, the Anti-slavery party held another election, and chose their own legislature and public officers. As might be expected, collisions ensued, which soon increased in number and violence, and the year 1856 saw something like a civil war, attended by cruel outrages and murders, raging in the heart of the Union. This was at length put a stop to, by the interference of the President, towards the close of the year. Though the government is said to have given peculiar encouragement to the Pro-slavery party, and Congress has long refused to give Kansas admission as a State, the settlers in favour of freedom now predominate, and it is understood that that territory will be admitted as a free State during the present session, 1860-61. (It has been admitted, at last, on Jan. 30, 1861.)

The overthrow of the Missouri Compromise, first by Congress, and subsequently by the Supreme Court, the violent proceedings in Kansas, and the endeavours of Congress and the Government to prevent that territory being admitted as a free State, to which she seemed entitled even by the Popular Sovereignty principle of their opponents, have only had the effect of rousing the Anti-slavery party to more vigorous efforts. These efforts have now been rewarded with success in the election of a man of their party to the high office of President, and the placing the power of the Government in their hands; and they have, it is believed, also been able to secure in Washington, Utah, and Nebraska, north of the Missouri Compromise line, a population favourable to their views; regions, however, for which, from the climate and products, negro slavery is not adapted.

The only remaining territories are those of New Mexico, in which there are a few slaves, and the Indian territory, both south of 36 deg. 30 min. It was at one time supposed that the former would be peopled by Anti-slavery settlers; but it has turned out otherwise; and early in 1860 the Territorial Legislature of New Mexico passed enactments not only sanctioning negro slavery, but authorizing all servants to be corrected by their masters for neglect of their duties as servants, provided " that such correction shall not be inflicted in a cruel manner with clubs or stripes." The House of Representatives, by ninety-seven to eighty-nine, passed a bill to declare these acts null and void, but it was thrown out by the Senate. If the slavery question were settled as to these two territories, there remains none other, in the present domains of the United States, as to which disputes could arise. But, from the disorganized condition of Mexico and Central America, the Southerners look to the acquisi-

o

tion of new territory in these directions, and will never agree to any compromise which would exclude them from introducing slavery in these regions.

The questions at issue regarding the black races have thus led to a contest, characterized by the fiercest hostility and bitterness, between two sections of the white race, the North and the South. Abhorring slavery as I do, and sympathizing heartily with every practicable measure for its extinction, it yet appears to me that the States of the North are in great part responsible for the present condition of this unhappy conflict and the bad feeling between the North and the South. United by a solemn compact in a great confederation, the citizens of the different States were bound by every consideration of good faith, humanity, and common sense to adhere to the terms of h at compact, and honourably carry out its stipulations, so long as the compact existed. If, as was very natural, the free States afterwards found reason to complain of the conditions of that compact, it was their part to recede, or make known the conditions on which they would abide by it. When the free States came to loathe the odious task assigned to them of delivering up runaway slaves, and desired that the curse of slavery should not be admitted into new regions, which they were able to people with free men, and in which they judged it right that only free institutions should be implanted, their course was clear: they should have given notice of their determination to withdraw from a Union which imposed an odious thraldom upon them, and to break a connection the conditions of which they found intolerable. This would have been a straightforward and honourable course, would have commanded universal respect, and would have been a deadly, yet legitimate, blow at the system with which they thus shrunk from holding communion.

Their forefathers made the compact for them at a time when the evil was one of far inferior magnitude; since that time, not only has the evil been enormously increased, but the progress of humanity has altered men's views regarding it, and they had a right to withdraw from sanctioning in any way an institution they felt as at once unjust and inhuman: or, if they had not, by the Constitution, the legal right of withdrawing (and that is a doubtful point), the actual right could not have been withheld from them; they are by no means scrupulous as to constitutional obligations, and, in fact, a little rebellion is quite constitutional in the New England States. But they desired to retain the advantages of the Union without fulfilling its stipulations, and to soothe their consciences at other people's expense. They *first* ruptured the Union by deliberate legislative enactments, interfering with the execution of the Fugitive Slave Law;—by violent denunciations of it, and declarations at public meetings that they would oppose it—proceedings which were pronounced by the most eminent lawyer and statesman of the North to be *distinctly treasonable.* With a blind or reckless disregard of the delicate and dangerous position of their brethren of the South, they have laboured to expose them by inflammatory speeches and harangues to the horrors of a servile insurrection. A subject requiring peculiar and gentle treatment has met the roughest handling from a large portion of the Anti-slavery party. Thus the slave-owners of the South have been maddened by the wild and incendiary proceedings of the Northern Abolitionists. Having this truly black inheritance handed down to them from their forefathers, and extended by the extraordinary development of the cotton trade, irritated by the insults and reproaches of the demagogues of the North, stung by the superior tone assumed towards them by those who have had the good fortune to be born free from this bad institution, enraged at the cool proposition of many to deprive them, without compensation, of their property and means of living, and trembling for the safety of their families from causes which Northern proceedings tend greatly to aggravate, we cannot be surprised that the South hates the North with a fierce hatred that has never been surpassed, or that the Southern States desire to secede and save themselves from the tyranny of an arrogant and insulting Northern majority. There is not, and cannot be, any union of feeling between them; there is an active and violent repulsion;—as stated truly by Mr. Seward, there can be no permanent compromise between parties so utterly opposed in principles and feelings. Secession seems an inevitable necessity.

Though long threatened, the first exciting causes of the recent secession feeling in the South were the long persistence in the attempt to force upon them, in the House of Representatives, a presiding officer peculiarly obnoxious to them, and the extraordinary sympathy exhibited by the North towards the leaders of the John Brown insurrection, at the close of the year 1859. I was in the United States at that time, and saw and heard of innumerable manifestations of that sympathy. They were "heroes," and "gallant martyrs," whose memory was to be revered for their brave efforts in the cause of freedom. That was much more offensive than the insurrection itself, which was the act of a few desperate men, led on by a half-fanatical leader. But the way in which the rising was received in the North showed a deep-seated feeling of hostility towards the South, widely spread through a great community. The Southerners never forgave that; they could not. It was a declaration of war against them. It was not confined to rabid speeches at meetings, or wild articles in abolition newspapers, or private subscriptions for Brown's family; it was manifested by many of the public authorities in the free States; and thus revealed a state of public sentiment that proved to the South that the North was their foe, feeling as a foreigner towards them, rejoicing in their dangers and afflictions, and lamenting the fall of those who would have stirred up a bloody revolution amongst them. In the message of the Governor of the State of Massachusetts, in the beginning of the year 1860, long passages were devoted to the subject of slavery, with its recent history, and the doings of the Pro-slavery party were enumerated and spoken of with great severity; but there was no condemnation of the Harper's Ferry insurrection, not even a regret; its leaders were mentioned sympathisingly as "persons who suffer from misfortunes, or are required to pay the penalties of the law," and a high eulogium was passed on the character of John Brown.— And yet Massachusetts wonders that the South does not love her, and desires to break off all communion with her.

In December, 1859, the Northern States were full of that wild, fanatical spirit on the subject of slavery; it has continued unabated ever since, and a twelvemonth later prompted an invitation to Lord Brougham, from Massachusetts, to cross the Atlantic Ocean, to celebrate the anniversary of the execution of John Brown, for endeavouring to raise a slave insurrection in the sister State of Virginia. It does not seem to have moderated, and in verifying the incautious words of the Republican leaders, Seward and Lincoln, that freedom and slavery are committed to an "irrepressible conflict," till one or other prevails, renders it not unnatural that the slave States of the South should desire to evade this conflict, to secure in time a position of independence, and to avoid being under the control of an offensive and impracticable party; to be free, instead of remaining in subjection to a majority, animated by the hostile spirit which has been made so manifest towards them, and which they have reason to fear might become aggressive when in command of power. Policy dictates secession; they desire to secure their peculiar institution from interference, and to spread it into new regions; they look to free-trade in the reduction or abolition of the duties on imports established for the benefit of Northern manufacturers, and they hope to raise up in the South great marts of commerce, like Boston and New York. On the other hand, besides the general disadvantages of having a foreign power on their frontier, secession exposes the slave States, as such, to peculiar risks; and their truest interest might be to bear a good deal, and still stand by the Union. But feeling, as well as policy, has a large share in secession. Their pride is wounded; having long been the ruling party, they feel humiliated at the prospect of being the minority; they could bear the taunts, reproaches, insults of a few abolitionists, while they had power in their hands, but now that it seems about to part from them, the thought of being ruled by a party so obnoxious to them, is a mortification too bitter to be endured.

The election of Mr. Lincoln was not the only cause of secession: this may be said to have been in progress more than twenty years. It was only the last feather that turned the scale; but it was an important one, not only as an evidence of a deep and wide-spread feeling, but as throwing the power and prestige of the Government into the hands of the enemies of slavery.

Matters seem now to have gone too far for reconciliation; and the South demands what the North will consider as high terms. To satisfy the slave-owners, they must have access to the Territories with their slaves so long as they are in the territorial condition; an efficient fugitive slave law; neutrality of the general Government as to the slave-trade between the States and slavery in the District of Columbia; and, perhaps, the right of retaining their slaves during temporary residence in, or when passing through any State. With less than these, they will feel not upon an equal footing with the people of the free States, at a disadvantage compared with them, and thereby humiliated. They are proud and high-spirited; it is too much to be feared that there can be no permanent adjustment. The Mahomedan does not detest the Christian, nor the Venetian the Austrian, with half the bitterness with which the South hates the North in the United States. No person who has attended to the course of this struggle, or read the recent speeches in Congress, can doubt as to the burning hatred with which the North is viewed by the South. With such feelings, with commercial interests at variance, with so much sovereign power retained by the individual States, and such a strong spirit of resistance to authority pervading the public mind, it is almost impossible to hope for the preservation of the Union, whatever may be done in the way of patching up a compromise. The Republican party will damage themselves in the eyes of a large body of their supporters, if they depart from their Chicago platform of 1860, which declared —

"That the new dogma that the Constitution, of its own force, carries slavery into any or all of the territories of the United States, is a dangerous political heresy, at variance with the explicit provisions of that instrument itself, with contemporaneous exposition, and with legislative and judicial precedent." (This refers to the Dred Scott decision.)

"That the normal condition of all the territory of the United States is that of freedom; that as our Republican fathers, when they had abolished slavery in all our national territory, ordained that 'no person should be deprived of life, liberty, or property, without due process of law,' it becomes our duty, by legislation, whenever such legislation is necessary, to maintain this provision of the Constitution against all attempts to violate it; and we deny the authority of Congress, of a territorial legislature, or of any individuals, to give legal existence to slavery in any territory of the United States."

It is difficult to see how, with this declaration of principles, the Republican party can accede to the proposed compromise of giving over to slavery all south of 36 deg. 30 min. north lat., reserving that north for freedom. With less than that, the South never will be satisfied.

While the legal right of the Southern States to secede is doubtful, and its policy still more questionable, one cannot but be amused at the very large talk about coercion, and the high tone in support of the Federal Government now assumed by the Northern States. It is, indeed, strange to hear the good people of the North denouncing the secessionists of the South as traitors and rebels, accusing them of treason, and great crimes against the State ; discoursing in a high-sounding style about crushing sedition, and giving themselves the loftiest airs, like potentates of a dynasty that had reigned a thousand years over one consolidated people. If we consider how recent the union between these States is, and how loose it is, how long they had previously existed as governments perfectly independent of each other, and the large powers of self-government left to the individual States at the union, we must perceive that, whatever may be the strict law of the question, secession is not at all like what is commonly understood as treason or rebellion, but rather to be considered as analogous to the withdrawal of one of the partners from a Company; and that a high-handed attempt at coercion is not the treatment suited for so very peculiar a case. But, setting that aside, for the people of New England to reproach the South with treason, is truly admirable! They practise a good many little treasons and some large ones themselves ; they have ever been ready to burst into rebellion when the Federal Government did anything to displease them. They had a little insurrection in the very infancy of their independence of Britain, in 1786-7 ; the famous Hartford Convention in 1814, and other Northern proceedings during the trying period of the second war with Britain, were as near treason and rebellion as possible, if they did not actually reach so far; and Rhode Island had a private rebellion of its own in 1841-2. This very secession, which they denounce as treason, has been in great part caused by the treason of Northern States in defying, by deliberate acts of their legislatures, the provisions of the Constitution, and of acts of Congress; and these high-handed crushers of sedition have openly expressed their sympathy with endeavours to raise insurrection in a sister State of the Union; they write and talk, and by their legislatures enact treason, but insist on having a monopoly of it; they live in an atmosphere of resistance to authority, but are quite shocked, and assume the magniloquent tone and severe aspect of a government founded on Divine right and established for centuries, when another State desires to exercise a little of that liberty of resisting which they have so long indulged in.

Quis tulerit Gracchos de seditione querentes.

The South will never submit to coercion. They have too much pride and too much courage for that; and they will have the advantage of the defensive, and of the patriotic feeling of resistance to invaders. They have a vast territory, of which the larger part is at a great distance from the resources of the North. It is earnestly to be hoped that force will not even be hinted at; this will only exasperate the South still more, and destroy the faint prospect which still exists of some amicable arrangement to preserve this great Union. To talk of secession as treason and rebellion in the ordinary acceptation of these terms, to be put down with the strong arm of the law, or the military force, is to shut one's eyes and ignore all the peculiarities of the case. If the North, puffed up with its newly acquired power, vain of its elevation to "sovereignty," and indignant that any of its anticipated subjects should refuse to pay it homage, ventures on war to reduce them to obedience, the result must still be secession, with the addition of a waste of blood and treasure, ruin to trade, and more embittered feelings than ever between those who might, though separate, still remain friendly and of mutual benefit to each other.

I have already quoted one distinguished Northern, an opponent of slavery, Dr. Channing. I think my readers will be pleased to see the views of another eminent Northern, well known on both sides of the Atlantic, Mr. Everett, as to the difficulties which surround this great question. He says, "Have those, who rebuke the South for the continuance of slavery, considered that neither the present generation nor the preceding one is responsible for its existence? The African slave-trade was prohibited by Act of Congress fifty-one years ago, and many years earlier by the separate Southern States. The entire coloured population, with the exception, perhaps, of a few hundreds surreptitiously introduced, is native to the soil. Their ancestors were conveyed from Africa in the ships of Old England and New England. They now number between three and four millions. Has any person, of any party or opinion, proposed, in sober earnest, a practical method of wholesale emancipation? I believe most persons, in all parts of the country, are of opinion that free labour is steadily gaining ground. It would, in my judgment, have already prevailed in the two northern tiers of the slave-holding States, had its advances not been unhappily retarded by the irritating agitations of the day. But has any person, whose opinion is entitled to the slightest respect, ever undertaken to sketch out the details of a plan for effecting the change at once, by any legislative measure that could be adopted? Consider only, I pray you, that it would be to ask the

South to give up one thousand millions of property, which she holds by a title satisfactory to herself, as the first step. Then estimate the cost of an adequate outfit for the self-support of the emancipated millions; then reflect on the derangement of the entire industrial system of the South, and all the branches of commerce and manufactures that depend on its great staples; then the necessity of conferring equal political privileges on the emancipated race, who, being free, would be content with nothing less, if anything less were consistent with our political system; then the consequent organization of two great political parties on the basis of colour, and the eternal feud which would rage between them; and finally the overflow into the free States of a vast multitude of needy and helpless emigrants, who, being excluded from many of them (and among others from Kansas), would prove doubly burdensome where they are admitted. Should *we*, sir, with all our sympathy for the coloured race (and I do sincerely sympathize with them, and to all whom chance throws in my way, I have through life extended all the relief and assistance in my power), give a very cordial reception to two or three hundred thousand destitute emancipated slaves? Does not every candid man see, that every one of these steps presents difficulties of the most formidable character, difficulties for which, as far as I know, no man and no party has proposed a solution?"

The preceding is from the speech of Mr. Everett, at the great Union meeting, held at Boston, on the 8th of December, 1859, in support of the Union, and to protest against the sentiments of the sympathizers with the recent insurrection in Virginia. One resolution stated—

"We regret that the main body of our citizens, too much through the neglect of their political duties, have been often falsely exhibited in the eyes of the nation by those whose councils and conduct do not command the general approbation."

When we consider statements such as these, by such men as Dr. Channing and the Hon. Edward Everett, and review the history of the slavery question, it will be seen that those who have set themselves forward as the friends of the negro are by no means so harmless and discreet, nor the other party so utterly wicked and unreasonable, as numbers in Europe seem inclined to suppose. As foreigners, we must naturally incline to be cautious in our judgments on a question involved in so many difficulties

P

and peculiarities, which it is not easy for us to appreciate. To our ancestors the fastening of this great evil upon the United States is due; we have only recently wiped out the stain from our own soil, and for us to do so was a comparatively light and easy matter; while, by our recent commercial policy, we have given no small encouragement to slavery. The Southern States, whether in a separate confederacy or in the Union, are in anything but an enviable situation, and, without abating our desire to see slavery come to an end, or at all approving of the conduct of the planters, some allowance and consideration for the difficulties and perilous position which they have inherited might be not altogether out of place.

The question of secession, now of such deep interest, does not appear to have been provided for by the Constitution, unless indirectly, in Article V., which treats of amendments to the Constitution. This article enacts that amendments must be *proposed* by two-thirds of both Houses of Congress, or by a convention of the people on the application of the legislatures of two-thirds of the several States; and that such amendments must be *ratified* by the legislatures of three-fourths of the States, or by conventions in three-fourths of the States, according as Congress may determine on one or other mode of ratification.

If these conditions are not fulfilled, there seems no other way in which secession can be constitutionally sanctioned; and, legally, Congress and the President are justified in the course which seems to have been resolved on by Mr. Lincoln, to ignore any act of secession not effected in the mode appointed by the Constitution, and to collect the duties and retake and hold the Federal forts in the seceding States, as if they had not seceded. Every one will sympathize with the new President and the Republican party in their desire to do all in their power to preserve the Union, which stands so great before the world, and has had so glorious a career. But the questions arise, can it be preserved by force? Are not the separate interests and feelings of resentment of the Southern States so powerful that there can be no real or beneficial union with the Northern States? Are they not so great and so determined that only a long, bloody civil war could subdue them, that result being even then doubtful? Do not the large legislative and governing powers possessed by the several States—Sovereign States, as they are termed

—and their different commercial and other interests, sanction in reason, though they may not in the strict letter of the law, their withdrawal from a union when it ceases to be a benefit to them?

Granting the general inadmissibility of a right of secession, are there not, in this instance, features quite peculiar, which set aside general rules? Is this a case for the rigid enforcement of the law, or one of those emergencies that rise above law, and demand an equitable adjustment solely upon their intrinsic merits? Mr. Lincoln is said to have taken for his model the conduct of General Jackson in 1832-3, when he declared his fixed resolution to employ force to collect in South Carolina the heavy protective duties imposed to favour the Northern manufacturers, and which she endeavoured to resist or nullify, as injurious to her interests. It is true that South Carolina deferred her resistance, and the determined front shown by the President seemed to prevail; but the nullifying State only delayed, in hopes of support from the other Southern States, or of relief by Congress from the duties complained of. By a compromise measure, devised mainly by the distinguished statesman Henry Clay, Congress did yield what satisfied the Southern party, and the nullification storm passed away. But opposing commercial interests still remain to separate North from South; and the fierce and bitter feud as to slavery is superadded.

CHAPTER IV.

AMERICAN CITIES — HOTELS — SCHOOLS — WOMAN IN AMERICA.

'Tis Education forms the common mind;
Just as the twig is bent the tree's inclined.

THE cities and the schools are the glory of the United States. Perhaps the people themselves, if asked, might give " the Constitution " as the greatest thing they have done. They boast of it a good deal, have a sovereign contempt for all other constitutions, and every American—man, woman, boy, and girl—seems able, and very willing, to give a long lecture on its manifold perfections. However, as we find that, notwithstanding many admirable provisions, evincing the care and judgment of its founders, it can hardly maintain law and order, and does not prevent the grossest political corruption, we must look elsewhere for something of which the people of the United States have a right to boast.

I think they may be proud of their cities.

Nowhere have I seen anything to equal them in neatness, cheerful aspect and general elegance. Compared with them, a city in the Old World is dull and dingy looking. No doubt, in the generality of the large towns in Europe, there are numerous fine old buildings which excite our admiration and interest; we cannot reasonably expect anything like them in the comparatively new cities of America. But it is not a fine building here and there which determines the appearance of a city: it is the character of the ordinary buildings—the houses and stores— which are everywhere. In the United States, these are so tasteful and elegant, and of such superior material, that it is quite a treat to walk along the streets, which have a highly rich, lively, and variegated appearance, from the variety of stone of which the houses are built, and the variety of beautiful architectural designs which they exhibit. Chestnut and Walnut streets, in Philadelphia; in New York, Broadway, and the streets which run from the lower part of it to the water—Fifth Avenue, and the streets in the vicinity; in Boston, Washington, Hanover, Franklin, and State streets, are perfectly magnificent. I have seen nothing worthy of being compared with them on this side of the Atlantic. The houses or stores are lofty, built of a rich red or fawn-coloured freestone, granite, marble, iron, or brick,—and always with some architectural decoration that pleases the eye, and interests and excites the taste of the observer. In no buildings erected in the leading streets within the last ten or twenty years do we find that hideous-looking structure so common in England—the dull, dead surface, with regular monotonous rows of windows, without any projection, curve, or decoration to break the stiff, flat, rectilinear uniformity; bare, miserable, and utilitarian in its aspect.

Chestnut Street in Philadelphia is certainly one of the prettiest streets I have ever seen. There is scarcely a plain, common-looking building in its whole length. Many of the banks and stores are of granite or marble; a new tasteful design meets the eye at every step; trees on both sides grace and enliven the view, and at one part, where the street widens, and the fine building, Independence Hall, rears its quaint old front, in strange contrast with the surrounding modern structures, the effect is remarkably pleasing. Independence Hall is the old State House; it is built of brick, apparently of the period of Queen Anne, or the early Georges, and has somewhat of the look of Chelsea Hospital. The room in which the famous Declaration of Independence was signed on the 4th of July, 1776, is shown; it contains a number of portraits of the signers, and a variety of interesting memorials of the event; and the polite and agreeable attendant in charge of it takes particular pleasure in pointing out all the curiosities to a Britisher. It is not only in the leading streets, public buildings, and large stores, that this taste for neatness and elegance is manifested in the architecture of Philadelphia; it is seen in the smaller streets and humbler houses in the suburbs; they are of brick, but with marble steps at the door, and a marble basement, which relieve the monotony of the flat surface, and give a lively, tasteful aspect to the street. The Quaker city is truly very unquaker-like, but looks, more almost than any city I have seen, bright, cheerful, and elegant. But let the visitor avoid the suburbs on a Saturday morning; then Philadelphia is cleaning itself. This it does with characteristic American energy, and there is such scrubbing, washing, and splashing at the door of every house, that it is best to be out of the way.

Certainly, architectural taste has made great progress amongst the Americans; and that taste does not develop itself in merely planting fine public buildings here and there—necessarily few and far between : it impregnates every-day life, and gives the people a pleasure in seeing the scenes of their daily work surrounded with forms of grace and beauty ; and, if continued for a very few years longer, will render each American city *a city of palaces*. In some instances the decoration is overdone, and there is a profusion of ornament ; but generally speaking, a very good taste prevails in the designs of the house and store fronts in the United States. I am told that the new cities in the West rather exceed than fall short of those near the Atlantic coast in their magnificence and ornate style of architecture.

Having seen a number of large cities of the Old World, I confess I was a little startled to find them so much eclipsed in architectural beauty by these comparatively modern towns of the United States. Nowhere have I seen a street at all to be compared with Broadway, New York, in grandeur and richness of appearance. This it owes to its breadth, the loftiness of the buildings, the fine material of which they are made (often a beautiful white marble), and the elegant and varied architecture. Regent Street, Oxford Street, and the Strand in London, as well as the Boulevards of Paris, must hide their diminished heads when contrasted with the great street of the commercial capital of the States. Manchester, Liverpool, Glasgow, and Birmingham look dull, dingy, and monotonous, when compared with Boston or Philadelphia. The smaller towns, too, have a clean, tasteful, and cheerful aspect. The suburban villas in such places as Fall River and Newhaven are singularly elegant; and the cottages of the workmen in the latter, isolated, and in the midst of a bit of garden ground, are remarkably neat and comfortable-looking. There are trees in most of the streets; the houses, whether of wood, stone, or brick, are, by some pretty design, and painting or whitewashing, made to please the eye; and in all the New England towns and villages there was a bright sunshiny look, that I could not but envy and admire.

The geology of a country has much to do with the character of its architecture. Where there is abundance of a material capable of receiving and preserving beautiful forms, there, sooner or later, they will arise under the hands of the sculptor and architect. The oolite in the vicinity of Bath, and the fine freestone near Edinburgh, have rendered these cities the most elegant in Britain. But a great part of England is in the tertiary formation, where clay is more plentiful than good building stone; and

as neither bricks nor outside coverings of plaster
are well adapted for architectural ornaments,
London and other towns in the middle and
south of England are, and will probably remain, inferior to most other cities in the appearance of the buildings. An architect in
Philadelphia told me that he considered that
city and Edinburgh to be the prettiest cities
he had seen. Everywhere, along the Atlantic
coast, fine building-stone seems to be at hand,
or easily accessible; and to this, in part, we
must attribute the superior appearance of the
cities. Some fine building material, freestone,
of a fawn or rose tint, is imported into the
United States, from New Brunswick and Nova
Scotia.

Another reason for the superior style of the
buildings in the American cities may be found
in the circumstance that, from the decay of the
previous wooden tenements, or the rapid extension of business, requiring them to be replaced
by larger structures, many houses and stores—
even whole streets—have been rebuilt within the
last few years; and everywhere, in both Britain
and America, there has been, within that time, a
decided re-action against the taste (?) for plain,
grim, ugly buildings which prevailed throughout the British empire from about the time of

William III. Nothing can be more elegant than the new parts of Edinburgh and Glasgow and of London (so far as brick and plaster will permit), or the schools, churches, villas, railway-stations, etc., erected in Britain during the last fifteen or twenty years. This happy revival of architectural taste has taken place also in the United States, and the fine building material and frequent opportunities for rebuilding have co-operated with this fortunate *renaissance* in adorning the cities of the great Republic.

Besides, the American is extravagant, and fond of having things about him handsome and stylish-looking. In matters of taste, go-a-head is still the rule; he likes show and dash, and to have his house, his furniture, his store, his equipage, his wife and daughters finer than his neighbours. Not only must he have his own private carriage elegant, but he will not ride in a poor, common-looking public conveyance. There is no cheap, handy cab or fiacre to be had in the American cities (or, at least, in many of them) like the one-horse cabs of London or Paris, that will take you a short drive for sixpence, and a long way for one shilling or one shilling and sixpence. Yankee scorns such a shabby-looking vehicle; his street conveyance is a huge thing, like a country gentleman's family

coach, very handsome, and drawn by two horses;
but for the honour of driving in which you
must pay extravagantly, so much so, that one
seldom thinks of it unless two or three are together, and one is going a long way. More
than once, when remarking on the want of some
small vehicle, the reply was, "Ah! that would
be a poor affair." In some of the large towns,
the want of this cheap cab is less felt—in certain
parts of the town, at least—from the very convenient street-railways, which are now laid along
most of the great thoroughfares.

The Americans have a somewhat unromantic
way of naming the streets in their towns by
numbers, or the letters of the alphabet, instead
of giving them the names of countries, rivers,
distinguished men, etc., according to the usual
method. But this plan of street nomenclature
is attended with very great convenience, particularly to a stranger. The greater part of an
American town having been planned out long
before any of it was built, the streets have been
arranged so as to be mostly at right angles to
one another. This is the case in Washington
with all the streets, excepting a few called
avenues, which cross the others obliquely, and
have the names of the States assigned to them,
as Pennsylvania Avenue, Massachusetts Avenue.

The other streets are denominated by numbers and letters. Those running east and west are A, B, C, D, etc.; those crossing them, in a north and south direction, 1, 2, 3, 4, etc. Thus, wherever you may be, you can find out exactly in a moment, by looking at the letters and numbers at the corners of the streets, which way you have to go to a street in any part of the town. Further, if a proper address has been given, you know how far you have to go, that is, to what part of the street. The address, 10th street, between F and G, or K (street), between 12 and 13, indicates, at once, the part of the street, or block of houses, for which you have to look. The same principle, though not so completely carried out, is found in other towns in the United States, as New York and Philadelphia. It is pleasing to find that the citizens of the United States have taken advantage of the newness of their towns to introduce this extremely convenient and useful mode of naming the streets; one more example, in addition to the numbers that meet one everywhere, of the ingenuity and eminently practical character of the people.

Several of the cities have admirable municipal arrangements, and publish yearly reports, exhibiting everything of interest regarding the condition of the city during the past year. One of the most complete and satisfactory of these is that of the city of Boston. A gentleman of that distinguished city favoured me with a copy of its *Forty-sixth Annual Report*, being for the financial year 1857-8. The following particulars, extracted from this volume—one of three hundred pages—may be interesting.

The revenue from ordinary sources, applicable to the payment of the current expenses of the city, was 2,303,050 dollars, of which 2,219,979 were derived from direct taxation. The population of the city in that year was nearly 170,000, which gives, therefore, a taxation of thirteen dollars per head, or £2 14s. sterling. The national taxation amounts to about two dollars per head, which gives fifteen dollars, or £3 2s. as the average amount levied in the form of taxes (direct and indirect) on every individual in Boston. Thus it will be seen that the people of that city, at least, are by no means lightly taxed. It must be observed, however, that poor-rates are included in the above, and that the citizens have the right, of which many avail themselves, of a free education for their children.

The taxes are essentially four—a *poll or head tax* of one and a-half dollars on every male resident citizen of the age of twenty or upwards, and taxes on *real estate, personal estate,* and *income from profession, salary, or trade.* The three latter are compounded into one. The personal estate consists of goods, merchandise, money, furniture, and plate in use above a thousand dollars in value, ships, mortgages, and moneys at interest more than interest is paid on, stocks of all kinds (except United States stock), horses, cattle, carriages, etc. The income-tax is charged only on the amount of income *over* 600 dollars.

Taxes are assessed on the combined value of real and personal estate on the following basis. If the person owns real estate to the estimated value of 5000 dollars, and personal estate valued at 3000 dollars, and his salary or other income from trade or profession is valued at 1500 dollars, he is taxed as follows:—

	DOLLARS.
Real estate, however much it may be mortgaged, at its full value	5000
Personal estate, same	3000
Income, 1500, less 600	900
	8900

	DOLS.	CTS.
Supposing the rate for the year to be 7 dollars on every 1000, his tax on real and personal estate and income would be	62	30
Poll tax	1	50
Total tax, dollars	63	80

Q

Thus it will be seen that the Bostonians, in their system of taxation, favour the man who lives on the precarious income dependent on his own life and exertions in two ways : *first*, in leaving 600 dollars of that untaxed; *next*, in assessing annually the whole value of all real and personal estate, instead of its annual proceeds.

From loans, bonds, and mortgages, and land sales 1,373,110 dollars were raised during the year, making the total revenue 3,676,160 dollars.*

The net expenditure was 3,371,042 dollars, including among others the following items :— Bridges, 26,117 ; fire department, 107,355 ; celebration of the 4th of July, 16,242; health and quarantine department, 107,708; houses of industry, reformation, etc., 102,541 ; the poor, about 60,000; police, 201,840; schools and ordinary repairs of school-houses, 345,519; streets, paving, lighting, etc., 417,644; contribution to the State tax, 337,915; public library building, 129,050.

THE AMERICAN HOTEL is a great invention, characteristic at once of the practical head, republican equality, and travelling propensities

* The rate of taxation had increased from 6 dollars per 1000 in 1847, to 9.30 dollars per 1000 in 1857.

of Brother Jonathan. It is simply the application of the co-operative principle to cheapen the expenses of travelling. A number of people agree to breakfast and dine together instead of separately, by which they can do so much more cheaply than if each ordered a separate meal for himself; and the landlord arranges the mutual co-operation for them, without giving the guests any trouble about it. The result is a great reduction in hotel expenses. In the best hotels in Boston you have everything you require, of the finest quality, and including ices and dessert after dinner, as well as servants' fees, and all in the handsomest style, for two and a-half dollars (about 10s. 6d.) per day; in others, equally good in every respect, but not so noted as fashionable resorts, for two dollars (8s. 3d.) per day; and I was in a hotel in Philadelphia where the charge was 6s. per day, the only material differences being, that there were negro waiters, and no ices; while there are some so low as 5s. or 4s. per day. Some hotels in New York, Washington, etc., charge 12s. per day; but in these, excepting a little more luxuriance in furniture, and the presence of a richer class, there is little advantage over those at two and a-half dollars daily, which is the general rate in the best hotels. In Boston,

I usually went to the AMERICAN HOUSE, at 8s. 3d. per day, where I had every comfort, every luxury I desired, so far as they could be had upon the American plan—a large, very handsome, well-conducted hotel indeed. Breakfast was going on from about seven in the morning till eleven o'clock, dinner from one to near five, tea from six to nine, and those who wished it could have a little supper besides from nine to twelve o'clock. There was a well-furnished bar, at which every kind of liquor could be had, or it might be brought to you at table. There was an excellent news-room, well stocked with papers from all quarters, a writing-room, a comfortable and handsomely furnished sitting-room for gentlemen, another for ladies and gentlemen with them, a visitors' room, and a large hall or lobby with well-cushioned seats, where you could sit and smoke, and be amused by the never-ending crowds going out and in.

At any of the hotels charging from two dollars per day upwards, abundance was supplied of the best articles, dressed in the best style. In the printed bill of fare for dinner at the American House, for January 9, 1860, there were, besides soup and fish, six varieties of boiled meats, three of cold meats, ten entrées, six roasts, besides a variety of vegetables, relishes, puddings and pastry, pineapple ice-cream, blanc-mange, nuts and raisins, etc. The other meals were in the same style. I mention these to show what is done in the United States, in hotels, by the application of the co-operative principle. I suppose that in England one would pay nearly double for the same extent of accommodation and entertainment. A hotel upon the American plan, with a restaurant attached, would probably meet with great success in any of our large towns.

The one advantage of the American hotel is its cheapness; in every other respect the English hotel is preferable. In the latter, you have a dining-room or a little side table, as the case may be, to yourself, which is your "Englishman's house is his castle" for the time being; you order what you please, when you please; you are not lost in a crowd; you are a great man; the waiter bows low, the landlord treats you with respect; they seem to be paying attention to you alone; you sit comfortably in your snug parlour or almost equally snug corner in the public room, and rest yourself after a meal, instead of hurrying out of a huge, dismal hall, which is merely a place for feeding in; you enjoy " mine ease in mine inn."

All this is very pleasant and very comfortable, but it has to be paid for. In the American hotel, on the other hand, you are nobody; the landlord is the great man, so great that he is seldom to be seen—you are merely one out of two or three hundred, "classed amongst creatures," as Byron says, must be at hand at the proper hours, are huddled in with the mob, get not always enough of elbow room, wait your turn in silence, for chit-chat is not encouraged, take what is provided for you and be thankful, hurry out immediately you have finished, no doubt with the wants of the animal machine supplied; but this is not "dining." It is unpleasant to those not "to the manner born;" but it is cheap.—The waiters in the best hotels are mostly Irish; in the others, negroes. The humble position of a waiter is below the dignity of a Yankee.

The number of large hotels, even in towns of but moderate size, is surprising, and shows that the Americans are greatly given to travelling. I am aware it is said that these hotels are not occupied by travellers only, but also by others—unmarried gentlemen, or families not inclined to incur the troubles of housekeeping. But the number of such parties is not great; and there can be no doubt of the locomotive propensities of the people of the United States.

In travelling along an American railway, even in winter, the cars are repeatedly almost emptied and filled again, and crowds are waiting at every station. Indeed, the cheap railway fares, comfortable cars, and moderate hotel charges, tempt people to travel: they have done so in the United States, and, doubtless, would have the same effect in this country.

Besides the large or public hotels, there are innumerable private hotels or boarding-houses in North America, which take the place of our "furnished apartments." These are extremely convenient. This arrangement is a very agreeable one for solitary persons, or couples without families, as well as for those who must practise economy. By this combination, one can command many more comforts and luxuries than in lodgings with the same means; and there is always some society to cheer one and help to while away hours that would otherwise be lonely. It is true, one cannot choose one's society in a boarding-house, and it might be supposed that many unpleasant encounters of temper and caprice must occur. But the people get used to the system, learn to smooth down their corners, and generally, so far as I could see or hear, live very happily together. I was told by an Englishman, who lived several years in a very respectable boarding-house, where there were some permanent residents and many coming and going for short periods, that, in all that time, he met only one who did not amalgamate pleasantly with the others. This was a crusty old gentleman who had a temper of his own. But he did not stay long; he left, ostensibly, because his dignity was offended by another gentleman, who had to go out early in the morning, getting his breakfast first; it was slyly hinted, however, that the seceder was jealous of the gentleman's attentions to his wife, a very agreeable elderly lady, nearer sixty than fifty years of age. Such are the droll occurrences that take place in boarding-houses occasionally. The boarding system in America greatly promotes the happiness and comfort of that large class of persons, especially females, who are left alone in the world, and who, in their own houses or in lodgings, have so many hours of dreary lonely pining. For such persons, for those with limited incomes, and for strangers in a place, the boarding-house is a very happy arrangement, that might, with great advantage, be more extensively introduced in this country. In North America the weekly charge for board varies from ten dollars to four, or even three dollars; seven dollars per week (£1 8s. 6d.) should afford every comfort, in a good style, and with the society of a well-educated, intelligent, and respectable circle. It is an evil in the boarding system that it sometimes tempts families to give up housekeeping, and the children are without a proper home or father's fireside; and there are yet other evils, which need not be referred to here. But it is attended with very great advantages for large classes, whose happiness and comfort it greatly promotes. The solitary furnished lodging of the Englishman, and the social boarding-house of the American are national characteristics.

American Schools. — Travelling in the United States is quite exhilarating; it is drinking in continual draughts of intellectual cordial. There is such a look of fire and intelligence in the people, such an activity and energy of business, so many clever contrivances, inventions, projects, and "notions," meeting one at every turn; so many conflicts of mind with mind, in which all partake; so many associations, public meetings, demonstrations; so many cheap papers and journals, instructing, arguing, asserting, denying, opposing; so noble, widely-diffused, and prominent a system of education for all classes, and in which all classes take a lively interest; and such an universal development of freedom, progress, and intellectual life, that one is forced to admit in the Americans a great, energetic, most intelligent, and original people, such as the world has never seen before.

Of the great doings of the people of the United States of America, the greatest and most honourable to them is their system of common schools. The universal diffusion of these schools, the liberal scale on which they are established and conducted, and their completeness and efficiency, render them the just pride, as well as the hope, and perhaps the safety, of the nation.

In the matter of education, the Americans exhibit no "ignorant impatience of taxation;" on the contrary, they impose upon themselves, and cheerfully submit to, heavy taxes for the purpose of educating the people. It is difficult to ascertain exactly how much they expend yearly upon their public schools; but as an approximation not very remote from the truth, it may be said, that a large part of the nation pays annually at the rate of a dollar a head for public education; or (if that rate were universal), thirty-one millions of dollars, nearly six and a-half millions of pounds sterling for the whole. The rate is different in different States—the north and north-west contributing most liberally to this great object. In the financial year 1857-8, Massachusetts, with a population of 1,132,369, raised by taxes for the promotion of education 1,341,252 dollars. In the same year, 1857-8, the City of Boston, with a population then of about 170,000, expended 345,519 dollars on schools and ordinary repairs of school-houses, being at the rate of two dollars per head. The City of New York, with a population of less than 800,000, in 1857, expended in that year 1,101,081 dollars on public education; of which 898,175 dollars, or more than one dollar per head, were raised by the tax on real and personal estate; the remainder was received from the State school-fund. In Philadelphia, 475,781 dollars were expended on public schools, in 1858, with a population of about 500,000. In the same year, the State of Ohio, with a population a little above two millions, laid out 2,739,837 dollars on educating its people; and Missouri, a slave State, in 1857, with a population of about 700,000, expended upwards of 630,000 dollars on public education. The ample means provided for education are derived partly from a State school-fund, originating in the school lands allotted for the purpose in the early stage of the settlement of the State, and partly from taxes. The State of Wisconsin, a compara-

tively new State, admitted to join the Union in
1848, now with a population of 600,000, had, in
1858, a school-fund of 3,107,484 dollars, giving,
at seven per cent., an annual revenue of 217,523
dollars, and being constantly increased by the
sale of school lands; and 334,000 dollars were
raised by taxation, for educational purposes,
during the year. Besides this, there was a
University fund of 316,365 dollars, the interest
of which at seven per cent. was applied for the
benefit of the State University at Madison.

The great majority of the youth of the United
States are educated at the public schools, and
these are now, in most districts, so very efficient, that some of the wealthier classes also
send their children to them. But I believe the
greater part of the latter are sent to private
schools. Parties connected with the public
schools seemed unwilling to admit this, as to
boys at least, though they allowed that the girls
of the better classes mostly received their education at private establishments. In 1858, in
eighteen leading towns in Massachusetts (Boston not included), 30,553 children attended the
public schools, at a cost to the State (exclusive
of any charge for school-houses) of 259,379
dollars, or eight dollars forty-nine cents. as the
cost of the instruction of each child. In the

same towns, in the same year, it was calculated that 2750 children were educated in 121 private schools, at a cost of 82,786 dollars, or more than thirty dollars for each.

The schools are generally *free*—there being no charge whatever; in many, even the schoolbooks are supplied gratuitously. In Baltimore, a charge of one dollar per quarter is made in some of the schools for more advanced pupils, books being liberally supplied; but free admission will be given to those whose parents are unable to pay; and, to the same class of persons, books will be given freely, in places where the custom is to let the pupils pay for their own school-books.

There are different arrangements in the different States; but, generally, there are three classes of schools—the *Primary*, for those under ten or eleven years of age; the *Grammar Schools*, for those from about ten to fifteen years of age; and the *High Schools*, for those from sixteen to twenty years of age: the latter is, in reality, a kind of college, at least for those who stay long enough to go through the complete course. Above these still are the *Universities*, such as Harvard College, near Boston; Yale College, in Newhaven. The following shows the annual cost for each pupil, furnished gratuitously by the public, in five of the High Schools :—

	Dollars.
Boston Latin High School	58
„ English High School	83
„ Girls' High and Normal School	43½
New York Free Academy	57½
Philadelphia High School	35

These differences depend partly on the reputation and success of the schools, the expense for each being less when the school is crowded, and partly on the different ideas of the managers as to the requisite number of professors and subjects of instruction.

The yearly cost of instruction per pupil in the lower schools (grammar and primary) was, in New York city, five and a quarter dollars; in Philadelphia, six and a quarter dollars; in the country districts it is somewhat less. The cost in the Boston primary schools is nine and one-third dollars; in the Boston grammar schools, eighteen and a half dollars.

The school houses are large, substantial, handsome-looking buildings, most completely supplied with every sort of educational furniture and apparatus, of good material. That great educational improvement, the single isolated seat and desk for each scholar (or one for two together) is adopted almost everywhere. This is attended with great advantages, isolating each scholar from the rest, and enabling him to come out of his place without disturbing the others. The expense is spared in *materiel* that will tend to make the school comfortable, agreeable, and efficient. In the estimated school expenditure for the city of New York, for 1858, I find 9000 dollars set down for the Ward (grammar) schools to supply them with pianos; in the expenditure of the year 1857, 689 dollars for instruments, apparatus, and chemicals for the use of the Free Academy of that city; and the State of Massachusetts, up to the end of the year 1858, had supplied to the schools throughout the country, for the use of the teachers and scholars, 3581 copies of Webster's large English Dictionary, and 116 of Worcester's, at a cost to the State of 14,556 dollars. Everything is on the most liberal scale: taste, and imparting a handsome, cheerful aspect to the school rooms, are consulted as well as efficiency; they are spacious, and almost elegantly furnished; and there is a clean, bright, lively look about them, that render them agreeable to the inmates, and pleasant to visitors.

The salaries of the teachers are different in different districts. The average pay of the male teachers in the State of Massachusetts (Boston included), is about 600 dollars, or £120 sterling per annum; of the female teachers, 235 dollars yearly, or .£47 sterling. In Ohio, male teachers are paid at the rate of 335 dollars per annum; females, 156 dollars. In some of the country districts they are not employed during the whole of the year. In the cities, the pay is much higher, and employment constant, or permanent at least. In the Boston *primary schools*, the teachers, mostly (or altogether) females, receive 390 dollars per annum. I have not been able to learn the exact average salaries, for the whole of Boston, of the teachers in the next higher class of schools, the *grammar schools*, but it is not far from 600 dollars. In the Dwight grammar school for boys, which I visited, there are two teachers, a master, an usher, and eight female teachers, and the total amount of teachers' salaries was 5760 dollars, (giving an average of 576 dollars), of which, no doubt, the two male teachers have the lion's share. I do not find in the Boston report any data for the salaries of the different grades of teachers in the grammar schools, nor in the report for the city of New York. But in these cities, the proportions are probably not very different from what they are in Philadelphia, as to which detailed information is supplied. In the grammar schools of that city, the usual arrangement is as follows: in a boys' school, with 275 on the books, and an average attendance of 255, there is a male principal, with a salary of 1200 dollars, and four female teachers, with, respectively, 350, 280, 260, and 240 dollars yearly salary. In a girls' school, with the same numbers, everything was the same, except that there was a female principal, with a salary of 600 dollars; that being the highest amount paid to any female teacher in the public schools of Philadelphia. In the secondary schools of that city, conducted entirely by females, the salaries are from 350 dollars, that of the principal, to 220 dollars; and in the primary schools, also conducted by females, from 300 dollars to 200 dollars, the latter being the lowest amount paid to female teachers in Philadelphia.

Female teachers, as must have been observed from statements already made, are much employed in the tuition of boys in the United States, and this tendency is rather on the increase. In Philadelphia, in the year 1857, of fifty-eight new teachers appointed fifty-seven were females. In New York, in 1858, of 1400 teachers in the public schools, 1200 were females, 200 males. The system is cheap, and seems to work well; the females appeared to have an aptitude for teaching, and good discipline was preserved. The services of an able, intelligent, well instructed woman may be procured at half the cost of those of a male, and for the junior schools her labours are nearly equally efficient; the Americans say, more so in certain cases, and have some fine-spun theories to prove that in this case what is cheapest happens also to be best adapted for the purpose. But there is no doubt that economy is the prime mover of the substitution of female for male teachers, which is now going on so extensively in the United States. In a number of schools, I had the pleasure of seeing female teachers of great ability indeed, who did their work thoroughly and well, several in quite a masterly style. Many were highly accomplished and very superior women. But I cannot say that they appeared healthy or happy: a careworn look was frequent. That prevails, in some degree, in all American women, but it seemed more marked amongst those engaged in teaching. Their labours are very valuable to society, and it is better for themselves to work than to pine and mope or starve; but still that is not their mission.

The schools are under the direction of a General Board of Education for the State, Dis-

trict, or City, chosen by the people, so many
committees having charge of certain school districts,
and others of certain subjects—as elections,
rules and regulations, salaries, accounts,
text-books, school-houses, music, etc. Boston
is divided into eighteen school districts, each
having a grammar school and a number of primary
schools, under the superintendence (subject
to the rules laid down by the General
Board) of a school committee of about six or
seven members. Few respectable men are to
be met with in any part of the United States
who are not, or have not been members of
some school committee; and these gentlemen
take great interest in their appointed work, and
are usually extremely well informed on every
thing relating to the cost, working, and general
condition of the schools under their control.
Thus, the whole of the more intelligent part of
the community is brought into direct acquaintance
and intimate connection with the school
system, which greatly contributes to its strength
and popularity, and to the public interest in it.
There is usually a superintendent of public
schools, with assistant inspectors, who visit
them frequently (which the members of the
committee do also), and submit reports to the
General Board.

In the Massachusetts public schools, there are 218,198 children on the roll in winter, or about 1 in 7 of the population; of these 12,370 are under 5 years of age, 16,894 above 15. It is believed that 74 per cent. of those between the ages of 5 and 15 years of age are in actual attendance at school.

I visited a great number of the schools—several more than once, and in some spent a considerable time. The general impression left on my mind was that the teaching was most thorough and efficient. I speak of the primary and grammar schools—those that train the great body of the population, which is always comprised in the class that leaves school before reaching sixteen years of age. In such schools, classics and geometry were not taught (the latter a little perhaps), and the great means of intellectual training were grammar and arithmetic, with algebra. These were made the instruments of most thorough mental exercise, grammatical analysis and the principles of arithmetic being explored to their depths, and the pupils being perfectly familiar with them in all their parts. Any teacher who has examined the very superior school-books on these subjects, published in the United States, will be satisfied that they are there taught in a very thorough manner. It is an admirable practice, very general in the American schools, to make the pupil go to the board and work out there himself the whole sum in arithmetic or algebra, or the grammatical analysis, explaining every step of the operation as he goes along; to draw maps on the board, or give demonstrations in subjects of physical science, drawing the necessary illustrations. Again and again, I heard girls of about eleven years of age and under, after having worked sums on their slates in rule of three, interest, fractions, etc., rise, and with their slates before them, describe the whole operation, with all the whys and wherefores, in masterly style; and all were alert, all anxious to be called upon. Not only is the common "mental arithmetic," working sums mentally, much practised, but that higher mental arithmetic, the study of the theory of the operation, is very much cultivated. It is the same with parsing, the same with such parts of physical science as are taught to them. A girl of about fifteen years of age stepped out to the board, and making the necessary sketches as she went along, demonstrated, by a variety of reasons, the earth's rotundity, in a clear and systematic style; in fact, she spoke like a book, as one might say. The girls exhibited remarkable composure, self-confidence, and freedom from embarrassment. This practice of giving out a subject, and making the pupil expound it entirely, without any aid in questions from the teacher, gives both command of thought and language, fixes the matter in the mind, and enables a visitor to see what the pupils know and can do. Both pupils and teachers seemed to be pleased to show off before the Britisher; but I was in too many of their schools, and too long, often arriving unexpectedly, and heard too many examined, for any "showing off" in the unfavourable meaning of that expression; and it certainly appeared to me that the work which these schools professed to do, is well and thoroughly done. As a native of the old country, both teachers and pupils evinced the greatest courtesy and good-will towards me. And their politeness and friendly behaviour, and the remarkable animation, intelligence, and ability exhibited, made those very pleasant hours indeed that I spent in the American schools. Frequently I was requested by the teacher, or a member of the committee, to say a few words. From all I could see or hear, there appeared to prevail, amongst both teachers and pupils, a very good feeling towards the "old country."

Besides the subjects referred to above, the

history of the United States and early British history are taught very fully in these schools; geography and elocution receive a large share of attention. All are taught algebra (girls as well as boys), and seem to like it and make great progress in it; it is introduced at an earlier stage than amongst us. All are carefully instructed in "the Constitution of the United States;" physiology is fully taught, and instruction in music is very general.

In the higher schools—those semi-colleges of the large cities—science, especially physiology, is much cultivated. In the Free Academy of New York there is a professor of chemistry and physics, and one of "natural history, anatomy, physiology, and hygiène;" in the Central High School of Philadelphia there are two professors, devoted to the same subjects; and in the Baltimore Central High School natural philosophy and physiology are prominent parts of the course of instruction. In these three institutions, also, there are chairs of mental and moral science. These are schools for general, not professional education, meant chiefly for youth from fifteen to eighteen years of age; and in these, as well as many others in the United States, the two subjects, physiology and mental science, seem to be especial favourites, and to occupy a large portion of the pupil's attention. It is interesting to notice that EUCLID is almost banished from the United States. Yale College, in Newhaven, was the only place at which I saw it enumerated amongst the text-books. The most usual substitute is the work of the distinguished French geometer, LEGENDRE; other condensed courses are in use, but all seemed to be based on the work of Legendre.

The schools being free, the liberal scale on which they are supported, the efficient and thorough character of the instruction given, and the characteristic energy which pervades every department, must, ere long, render the people of the United States by far the best educated nation in the world. Nor is it merely a common or elementary education which is thus extended freely to all; those who desire it can enter the more advanced institutions, and pursue their education, in the highest branches, up to nineteen or twenty years of age, or further. The capacities and peculiar aptitudes of all, even of the poorest, are called forth. To the American people, education, in all its stages, is free as the air they breathe.

Although the Americans generally take great pride and pleasure in their public school system, there is no want of objections to it. Some hold that it is too costly, blame it as extravagant, and as a public burden that will not be borne, at least to the same extent, and complain that the schools are much too good. Probably these complaints emanate mainly from those who send their children to private schools, and who finding heavy charges there, and seeing the very efficient education given in the public schools, are a little out of humour at being taxed for the support of the latter. But now that it has taken root it will be difficult to effect any reduction that would render the schools less efficient. The great middle and lower classes have the power in their hands, and the taxes they pay are as nothing compared with the return they receive in a superior education, free, for their children.

It is also urged " that the public schools are worse than valueless—injurious to the morals and fatal to the religious interests of the pupils, and that the alleged deterioration in the morals of the community is justly chargeable to the public schools."—" That the frightful increase of lawlessness, violence, and crime which is apparent in our midst is attributable, to a very great extent, to the legalised absence in our institutions of religious teaching and Christian and moral discipline."—*New York Sixteenth Annual Report of the Board of Education*, 1858.

The Board, in remarking upon the subject, refers the alleged evils to "the principles of trade, as more recently taught, by which it is given up to free selfishness and competition; the doctrine practically set up that national wealth is the highest national good; the tactics of political parties, so full of temptations to evil; the wonderful activity with which crimes, and even the rumours and suspicions of crimes, are sought for and gathered up, painted in vivid and romantic colours, and spread before the whole people every day in the columns of our able and interesting newspapers;" and another cause, "more powerful than all other causes put together, the thousands of idle and ignorant children who never enter a school;" to remove which, industrial schools, under the direction of the various religious denominations, are recommended.

It is probable that these charges against the schools are somewhat exaggerated; but, on the other hand, the replies do not seem altogether satisfactory. Two important considerations are not referred to, *first*, that any school can do but little to implant religious principles; and *next*, that secular or non-sectarian schools do least of all.

That education forms the common mind is true only when the word is taken in a large sense, as including all the influences that operate on the minds of the young; school education is but one of these, by no means the most powerful, quite inferior in force to the home and parental influences. If the Americans are a religious people themselves, their children will probably grow up religious also, but not otherwise. Religion in the young is derived from home, from the church, from the Sunday-school, very little from the day-school, where implanting information and cultivating the intellect must ever be the great work; while the crowd, the bustle, the influence of the youth on each other, and the but weak moral power of one whose influence does not operate through the affections, and of whose actions little is seen, prevent any very impressive religious effect being produced. But if any day-school can do but little towards promoting religious feelings, still less is in the reach of the non-sectarian school. The abstraction which we may term Christianity *in general* has a tendency to be no religion in particular. When every sectarian principle is removed, the residuum is apt to prove but a *caput mortuum*, with little rousing or vivifying effect. A passage of

Scripture read in the morning, without note or comment, the routine daily repetition of the Lord's Prayer and the Commandments, moral injunctions by the teacher, "songs imbued with the purest principles of Christian morality," have but little influence compared with the daily systematic teaching of a Church Catechism, enforced and impressed upon the heart by the energy of a lively faith and earnest convictions; by the enthusiasm and authority of a great religious institution holding a prominent place in the everyday lives and affections of those who surround the child, mingling with all it sees and hears; the frequent visits of the clergyman and elders, the connection between these and like home and church influences, mutually sanctioning and strengthening each other. The education together of children of different sects has many beauties and advantages, but, for any religious effect, is quite feeble; and it is useless expecting the secular school to compete with the sectarian one in this respect. If the Americans wish their schools to do something towards training up their youth religiously, they must bring them under an energetic sectarian influence. But they will not do that; the being open to all sects is a vital principle with them; then their only hope must be the example of their own religious lives, the influence of the church, the pastor, and the Sunday-school.

If it be true, as alleged by some of the Americans themselves, that there is a "deterioration in the morals of the community," we may, perhaps, find the chief causes of this in the excessive development of freedom of thought and action, and impatience of control, which pervade the whole American system, rather than in the schools. Though commencing with political liberty, and a spirit of resistance to laws and public authorities, the tendency of these is to pass to excessive individual liberty in other things and impatience of every kind of restraint; and from many things which occur in the United States, there appear some grounds for the opinion, that the extent to which freedom from restraint by public authorities is carried, is leading, in all classes, to an inclination for freedom from moral restraint. When, with the pride in being free, there is conjoined the pride of intellect, so highly developed by the schools, the press, and the political system of the United States, it is not impossible that there may be a general weakening of the force of those moral influences and checks, which, in communities less advanced politically and intellectually, have so powerful an effect for good. If these be causes of the moral deterioration referred to, they will be by no means confined to the United States, though pushed much further there; for we are all tending in the same direction in which the Americans, by their liberty and equality, and immense energy, are far a-head of other nations. Connected with this subject is the curious result said to have been found in some of the states of continental Europe—that crime is not less, but rather more frequent, in those places where education and intellectual development have been pushed furthest.

If well founded, it is a serious objection to the management of the American schools, that the health of the children is injured by excessive work. It is very difficult to judge as to this; several medical men of eminence in the United States have asserted that this is the case; but the tremendous energy of the people, and the competition between the several schools, soon cause these warnings to be forgotten or neglected. In some places, I heard, the committees had forbidden lessons being given out for home study; which, however, will be a great loss as to the development of a power of self-education. I should think that many young girls in these schools are so much confined, and have their brains so taxed, not only by much work, but by being early pushed too far forward, as to injure the health of both themselves and future generations. I have seen not a few little girls much concerned with the consequences which flow from the product of the means being equal to the product of the extremes ; or with the constitutional course of procedure of the President in vetoing a bill, who, as I imagined, would have been much more advantageously occupied with their dolls, hoops, or skipping-ropes. These are difficulties we are all perplexed about. The true solutions seem to be, not sending children so early to school, and when they are sent, for a considerable time placing them there only for two or three hours daily, instead of the long oppressive six hours. But this implies mothers able to educate their children in their early years, willing to do so, and not looking upon the school as a happy means of getting rid of them.

In the United States, as well as in the provinces of British America, the Roman Catholics seem dissatisfied with the public schools, and desire to have their share of the public school fund, to establish separate schools in which their youth may be brought up according to their own religious system. In Boston, lately, there was a disturbance in one of the public schools, arising out of this question. The Catholic children had been instructed not to repeat the Ten Commandments, nor join in the Lord's Prayer. " There was a general disturbance and disorder in the different school-rooms during the usual reading of the Bible. The boys scraped with their feet, and made much disturbance by whistling and muttering; they afterwards all refused to say the Lord's Prayer, or recite the Ten Commandments." The father of one of the boys who was punished for this misconduct, made a complaint in the police-court against the teacher who had inflicted the punishment; but the latter was supported by the court. In New York, also, there is much trouble on this subject, and in some of the schools the religious exercises had to be omitted. These are of so very slight and general a nature, that they can hardly give a leaning towards, or from any religion at all; but the Catholics wish their religion taught to their youth at school, and for this purpose desire separate schools. It is natural that they should wish this, as the tendency of free intermixture with the other children during their school career is to weaken the force of Catholic principles in the minds of the children of that community. It has been said that numbers of the families of Catholic emigrants, in the third generation, are found to abandon the old faith. The emigrant himself remains steadfast; his children, brought up under the influence of his faith and zeal, conform at least; but the accumulating influence of the heretical atmosphere of America, tells upon the next generation. The Americans, however, are proud of their non-sectarian schools, and the educational boards have steadily resisted every endeavour to make them swerve from the plan they have laid down.

Woman in America.—The New World has not been more successful than the Old one in finding the solution of the great woman-problem—How to procure for woman that situation in life for which nature evidently designed her, but which so many women are unable to attain, and in default of which we find so much bad health, vice, or listless pining among the fairer portion of the human race. But the eminently practical genius of the United States, if it has not found the means of removing the evil, has freely opened the door for palliations, and made important steps towards lessening it, by giving women access to employments, that afford them at once the means of becoming independent, and of having some useful work with which to occupy and interest themselves. They are beginning to be employed in printing offices, as clerks, and at the Smithsonian's Institution, at Washington, I found a female engaged in this capacity. They are extensively employed as teachers, of boys as well as of girls; and the medical profession has been opened up to them, not only with advantage to themselves, but, it is said, greatly for the benefit of society, that finds, in the peculiar aptitudes of females, the supply of certain wants that had been overlooked or not sufficiently attended to.

At Philadelphia, I visited the *Female Medical College of Pennsylvania*. This institution was established in the year 1850, and up to the end of the seventh session, upwards of 150 female students had matriculated at it, some desiring to pursue the complete course and take the degree of M.D., others merely desiring to attend particular classes. The candidate for the degree must have studied medicine for three years, attended two courses of lectures on each of seven leading subjects specified, presented a thesis of her own composition and penmanship, and passed an examination by each of the professors. The cost of instruction for the whole course, and of the graduation fee, amounts to 175 dollars. Seven ladies graduated in the sixth year; four in the seventh year. There are seven professorships, two filled by females. Ann Preston, M.D., is Professor of Physiology and Hygiène; Emeline H. Cleveland, M.D., Professor of Anatomy and Histology, and Demonstrator of Anatomy. In her valedictory address for the session 1857-8, Dr. Ann Preston says, "The question of the *success* of woman as physician is not now an open one. Her success is already a matter, not of hope or of prophecy, but of history. That women, as well as men, who are unqualified and incompetent, have entered the ranks, we cannot deny; but there are medical women, in practice, amply sustained pecuniarily, who walk daily amid the benedictions of those whom their skill and knowledge have relieved." Professor Emeline Cleveland, in her introductory lecture for the session 1858-9, states, "It has become an established fact, that women shall henceforth form a part of the medical profession, and though prejudice has not yet entirely worn away, we are most happy to know and to assure you that its strength has departed; that the popular mind is apprehending the need of enlightened, intelligent female physicians; that the public press is on the side of our enterprize," etc. So far as I could ascertain, these statements of the learned professors are not without foundation. In Philadelphia, and in some other places in the United States, there are very respectable, regularly educated female physicians in considerable practice. I asked one or two medical men their opinions on the subject, but they did not seem to like it, and talked rather disparagingly of the movement. Everything new has a charm for the Americans; but as this novelty seems to be getting a footing, the following extract from the appeal of the governors of the above college for support, may be interesting :—

" They find the demand for female physicians wide-spread and increasing, and regard the study and practice of medicine as peculiarly adapted to the nice perceptions of woman, and the tenderness and refined graces of her nature.

" They consider that woman, as a wife and mother, pre-eminently *needs* a clear understanding of the functions of the human body and the means of preserving health ; and that hightoned and intelligent female physicians, from their relations to their sex, must be most important instrumentalities in imparting such knowledge, where it is most needed and will do the most good.

"It is well known that there is a vast amount of suffering among women, which is left without relief, from the shrinking delicacy of its victims; and it is therefore a demand of humanity that women should be put in possession of the requisite knowledge to administer the required treatment in such cases.

"They also desire a scientific medical education for woman, because it will furnish her honourable and profitable *employment*—giving her a new sphere of usefulness and happiness, where duty and the sympathies of her nature lead her—in the chambers of the sick and suffering."

The American independence, freedom, and impatience of control, have, as might be supposed, operated more powerfully in changing the character of the female than that of the other sex. Under the influence of the ideas of liberty and right of self-control, which prevail in America, woman seems there to be undergoing a serious change in character and social position. A great experiment is going forward, of the probable results of which it is difficult to judge at present. She claims the right to more extended fields of employment, which is being conceded to her: and certainly, by her energy and ability, she is proving herself well qualified for a variety of occupations, from which she has hitherto been excluded. She demands laws which will place her property and earnings under her own control when married; these, in some States, she has obtained, or is in the course of obtaining. In March, 1860, the Legislature of the State of New York passed an enactment extremely favourable to her in this respect. It declared all real and personal property, belonging or bequeathed to her, to remain her sole and separate property, not subject to the control of her husband, nor liable for his debts, except such as have been contracted for the support of herself or their children; allowed her to dispose of her real estate without his consent, on showing cause before the county court; made her absolute mistress of her personal property, and joint guardian of the children with her husband, with equal rights and powers. Many say this act has gone too far, and that the immense constituency of henpecked husbands in the State of New York were ably and too faithfully represented in the last Legislature. She claims, also, in the Woman's Rights Conventions, the right to vote, to enter the Legislature, and to be released by divorce from a permanently discordant union. Some go still further, according to the statements in an extraordinary article, by a physician of standing in New York, on the Causes of the Present Decline of American Women, which appeared recently in the " Knickerbocker Magazine." Of all the new ideas, projects, notions, to which the excessive liberty, inventive spirit, and go-a-headism of the United States give rise, none are more startling than those relating to woman.

There seems to be an increasing tendency to facilitate the obtaining of divorce, particularly in the Western States. At the Tenth Woman's Rights Convention, held not long since, resolutions were passed, but not unanimously, to the effect that, as men make serious mistakes in the selection of partners in business, teachers for their children, ministers of religion, legislators, and the same weakness and blindness must attend in the selection of matrimonial partners, " the dictates of humanity and common-sense alike show that the latter and most important contract should be no more perpetual than either or all of the former." Dr. W. F. Channing, of Massachusetts, states, " I found, at once, that a broad line divided the Eastern and Western policy with regard to marriage and divorce."—" At the West, the doctrine was substantially held, that it is the duty and interest of society to release the parties to a permanently discordant union."—" In becoming a citizen of Indiana, I sought release from an oppressive obligation, already null in its essential human conditions. I sought and obtained this release for its own sake, as a matter of personal and social duty. I did not seek it 'in order to marry a new affinity.' At the same time I reserved to myself the right to marry whenever I considered it conducive to my own welfare, having also due regard to the welfare of others." He considers the continuance of marriage, when there is a permanent mental unfitness for union, as the cause of great social misery and evil.

Wendell Phillips, of Boston, a clever but eccentric speaker, and well known as a violent abolitionist, is also a prominent advocate of the emancipation of that other slave, as he considers her, woman. The following extracts from reports will convey some idea of the doctrines of this champion of the fair sex :—

" You have granted woman's right to be hanged, therefore you must grant her right to vote. No class is safe unless government is so arranged that it can protect itself. That is the essence of democracy, and the corner-stone of progress. This republic admits the principle that the poor are not to be protected by the rich, but that they are to have the right and the power to protect themselves. Each class is to hold the sceptre in its own hands.

"He claimed for woman something more than to merely live in a house and 'look pretty.' This is a one-sided civilization, and is to be banished as soon as possible. Take a woman who is married; she amounts to nothing, only to look after a child or care for a parlour. But let her lose her husband, and be overtaken by poverty, and she soon develops the powers within her in a broad and successful life.

"By what right do you make woman a mere incident to man? The central idea of the whole matter is the right of woman to vote. She is to have the ballot box as her A, B, C. Women should enter more generally into government matters, as her presence was needful to the settlement of such questions as slavery and war. We don't want a world which is all trees, or all land, or all water, but a proper quantity of each. Let her have the ballot box and the opportunity to labour. Fill her mind with education and literature as you do man's. Make her a writer, thinker, speaker, a scientific investigator; give her something to do with her head, heart, and hand, and the world will achieve a height not yet attained," etc.

In the United States, the freedom conceded to all gives woman more scope for the development of her talents and capabilities. This, with the very superior education given in the common schools, in which the females have their full share, and the still higher education in the more advanced colleges for females now springing up,* will raise up a class of extremely smart, clever, and intelligent women amongst all classes of society. They are trained early to talk and think, to expound, demonstrate, and lay down the law on every subject. They are growing up very well informed, very intellectual, and very independent. This may not be favourable for the unfolding of the submissive charms; but it would be a little unreasonable and somewhat cruel to exact submission from females, when all around them are practising and enjoying independence, and the right of resistance. In beauty and elegance, as is well known, the

* The Legislature of Illinois lately chartered a " Female Aid Fund Association, in connection with a female college at Chicago," to establish by "contributions, bequests, lectures, and otherwise, a fund to assist all such worthy and needy young ladies as may apply, in acquiring a complete scientific or classical education, and thus qualify themselves for the highest stations within the sphere of woman."

women of the United States compare favourably with those of other nations; in intellectual development and accomplishments they will soon have no superiors. They do not appear healthy, however, a point which is now engaging the anxious consideration of American physiologists. In the following little sketch, I am glad to shelter myself under the protection of an American writer already quoted :—
" American women are too formal and statuesque; they carry themselves with a hauteur, as if they were entitled to homage, without giving anything in return. They will turn out a full omnibus of men, or a score of male worshippers from their church seats, without deigning to give in return the cheap courtesy of a smile or a bow, or the small change of ' thank you.' "

CHAPTER V.

NOVA SCOTIA.

"Acadie, the home of the happy."—LONGFELLOW.
"No one who has not witnessed it can imagine the bitterness of party feeling in this colony, or the virulence of the language in which it is expressed."—THE GOVERNOR OF NOVA SCOTIA.

THIS little province is one of the most recent acquisitions of Britain, though her claims upon it date from an early period. The peninsular part, or mainland, was ceded to the British by France at the treaty of Utrecht in the year 1713; and the adjacent island of Cape Breton was acquired, along with Canada, at the close of the Seven Years' War, in 1763. Systematic colonization by the British was begun in 1749, when a body of emigrants from England settled at Chebucto, a fine harbour on the Atlantic coast, and gave the name of HALIFAX to the town they founded there, in honour of the Earl of Halifax, president of the Board of Trade and Plantations. The area of the peninsula is about 15,600 square miles, and that of Cape Breton 3000 square miles. In 1850 the population of the former was 221,239; of the latter, 54,878; in all, 276,117.

Nova Scotia has a motley population; Scotch, English, and Irish emigrants; French, descendants of the old settlers; a few descended from American loyalists, who left the United States in 1783, when peace was established between Britain and her revolted colony; and some of German extraction. The latter are settled at Lunenburg, where German is still spoken; in Arichat, in Isle Madame, near Cape Breton, three languages may be heard, English, French, and Gaelic; and there are many from the Highlands of Scotland in Cape Breton Isle. The Roman Catholics are the largest religious body in the province, numbering about 70,000. The Church of Scotland in this province was a large and influential body, till broken up by the great feud about patronage, which caused the disruption of the established Church of Scotland in 1843, and spread, with no less bitterness and violence, to the Colonies, where there was no patronage. The Baptists are about 42,000, the Church of England a little less than 40,000. There are also about 24,000 Methodists, 28,000 Antiburgers, and a few Congregationalists, Lutherans, and Universalists. Grand Pré (now Horton) on the Basin of Minas, or Bay of Fundy coast, was the scene, in 1755, of a sad and celebrated event—the expulsion of numbers of the French Acadians from the country. They were suspected of assisting the French in their contests with the British in America, then commencing, and were forcibly torn from their homes, to the number of several thousands, and dispersed through the other British colonies, families being in some cases separated, never to meet again. This has been taken as the foundation of Longfellow's beautiful tale, "Evangeline."

> "Wives were torn from their husbands, and mothers,
>   too late, saw their children
> Left on the land extending their arms, with wildest
>   entreaties."

THE CLIMATE of Halifax, and indeed of the whole of the Atlantic coast of Nova Scotia, is very peculiar, one of the most singular, I should suppose, on the face of the globe. In England, we are accustomed to regard our climate as extremely fickle; but the changes here are perfect constancy compared with those on the east side of Nova Scotia. We might expect it to be so on considering the geographical position of this little peninsula. It is in the very debateable land of climate, where a variety of opposing forces meet; now one prevails, now another overcomes it, to be soon overthrown in its turn. In that region, the battle of the climatic influences is continually raging, and if any one wishes to set up as an oracle on the much vexed question of the weather, let him confine himself to the prediction, that "we shall have a change soon." Nova Scotia lies on the parallel 45 deg. N. lat., midway between the Equator and the North Pole, and thus is on the very battle ground between tropical and polar influences; it is on the margin of a great continent, characterized by severe cold during the great part of the year, and considerable heat during the remainder, and it borders a vast ocean, temperate during all the year; it receives some of the genial influence of the great gulf-stream, which passes it at a short distance, while it is chilled by the Arctic currents which skirt the coast in their southern course, and by the large body of ice so long pent up in the Gulf of St. Lawrence. Where so many hostile powers encounter one another, there must be a turmoil.

During four months, December to March both inclusive, the weather is almost continually oscillating between severe frost and thaw. For a great part of that time, besides minor changes, there is a decided change from frost to thaw, or the reverse, about *every three days* on an average, one kind of weather seldom continuing above a week, while, occasionally, there are three or four changes in that time. I have sometimes seen the thermometer at about 15 deg. below zero, between seven and eight in the morning, and, in a day or two, at 50 deg. in the shade about noon. Heavy snows fall at times; soon there is a warm wind from the south, the streets of Halifax are one mass of slush, and it is hard and disagreeable work to go but a short way along them. At other times, when the snow has lain a little, the surface, melted slightly during the day, is frozen at night, and the streets are a smooth field of ice; when in this state, not unfrequently, wind and rain supervene; the streets being steep, the ice and rain giving a very slippery basis, and the wind blowing one about at its pleasure over this unstable bottom, it is quite a feat to get home at all; to arrive without a few falls is a great performance. Many wear *creepers,* with little spikes, on their feet. Notwithstanding these frequent and violent changes, there is reason to believe that Halifax is a very healthy place. The inhabitants do not concern themselves with statistics, but the military find it a healthy station.

A season like this is called an "open" winter. Now and then, a Canadian, or, as it is called, an "old-fashioned winter" occurs, when there is steady frost, with a few heavy falls of snow about Christmas, which is cleared off the side-walks, and remains piled up the greater part of the winter. Such winters and heavy falls of snow are said to be much less frequent than formerly; this seems to be the universal testimony of all the "oldest inhabitants," and, I presume, must be accepted as an established fact. Some attribute this change to drainage, and the clearing of forests going on in British America; but when we consider the vast extent of that country, the great climatic influences of that immense tract of land, and of the ice-movements and currents in the adjacent seas, it seems difficult to imagine that so slight a cause could have any material effect, side by side with powers so great.

Although the weather is so severe and so changeable, there seems more sunshine and more blue sky to be seen in Nova Scotia in winter than in Britain; occasionally, also, even during frost, there is a balmy, delicious feeling in the atmosphere that makes one quite enjoy the open air. In such a state of the air, on a moonlight or starry night in winter, during hard frost, I have seen the audience coming out from an evening lecture, go a-walking instead of going home, and stay out an hour or more. At times, on such occasions, the trees, on every branch and twig, are coated with ice, and the moon's rays striking upon these natural lustres, produce a beautiful effect, especially if there is a slight breeze to set them in motion.

Fogs prevail during a great part of the year, though not extending far inland; they are most frequent during the long ungenial spring, from April to June, during which there is much ice on the coast, drifting south. These mists render navigation somewhat precarious: four ocean steamers—the Columbia, the Humboldt, the Indian, and the Hungarian, have been lost on the fatal shores of this small peninsula. The Nova Scotians, having heard of the dark, dense fog that envelops London for a few days towards the close of the year, have concluded that we live in continual fog, and seldom get a sight of the sun. They would not believe that I had seen more fog in six months in Halifax, than in six years in Britain. But there is certainly more cloud in the latter country. Putting fog out of consideration, there seems to be more sun and sky to be seen during the year in Nova Scotia than in this country. The sky is of a deeper tint, and moon and stars seem brighter than in England.

Halifax is nearly 7 deg. south of London, and hence, in winter, enjoys a more elevated sun, which also remains longer above the horizon; yet the winter temperature of the former, 24 deg. Fahr., is about 15 deg. below that of London, a striking illustration of the effects of oceanic currents, position as to land and water, and of an eastern coast in temperate latitudes. So near the Atlantic ocean, and nearly surrounded by water, the heat is seldom great in summer. The mean temperature for the whole year is 43 deg., about 6 deg. below that of London. Halifax has a much more temperate climate, in both summer and winter, than Montreal or Quebec, where the summer heat and winter cold are extreme. The average summer heat of Quebec is 68 deg.; of Halifax, 61 deg. The winter temperature of the former is 14 deg. As far as regards climate, I should suppose that emigrants from Britain would find Nova Scotia preferable to most other parts of British America.

Halifax is prettily situated on an acclivity which rises gently from the water side to an eminence called Citadel Hill. This is strongly fortified; and, from the summit, there is a very

fine view of the surrounding country, with the
harbour or basin penetrating seven or eight
miles further up, the banks of which are wooded,
and variegated by gentle undulations and pro-
montories, that make a pretty intermixture of
land and water in the scenery. At the shores,
the ground dips somewhat abruptly, and gives
deep enough water for large vessels at all states
of the tide. Those of the merchants who are
fortunate enough to have sites adjoining the
water have, perhaps, as pleasant offices as any
place in the world affords. The wharves, supported on piles, shoot out a little into the
water. The store or place of business is on the
shore end of the wharf, and the merchant steps
from it in a few seconds to his vessel lying at
the other end, and has, at the same time, if he
chooses to look at it, a very pleasing view of
the fresh blue waters and the opposite coast.
Placed on so fine a harbour, with deep water
at all times, which is seldom frozen and never
very rough, the nearest port to Europe on the
mainland, and in the centre of the great fish
region, Halifax has no common commercial
capabilities, and will, if connected by railway
with Canada and the United States, be the seat
of a very large transit trade. Indeed, its trade
is already great. Its imports, in 1859, amounted

to £1,261,901 sterling, of which about half a million were from Great Britain, a third of a million from the United States, £187,860 from British America, £25,408 from the British West Indies, £197,619 from other countries, as Cuba, etc. Of the British goods, cotton, linen, silk, and woollen manufactures, amounted to a quarter of a million. Of the imports from the United States, wheat, flour, corn, and cornmeal, leather and leather manufactures, pork and hams, and tobacco, were the largest items. Molasses, to the amount of £11,700, formed the chief import from the British West Indies; codfish (£77,380) and herrings (£31,393) from British America; molasses (£78,742) and sugar (£87,890) from other countries.

The exports amounted to £874,243, of which the leading items were as follows :—

Codfish	£249,884
Mackerel	105,589
Herrings	104,401
Sugar	55,794
Molasses	49,785

Also furs (£10,754), lumber (£6,408), oil (£23,712), oats and barley (£13,274), and other fish (alewives, lobsters, scale fish, salmon) about £38,000. The largest portion of these exports (£281,245) is sent to the other parts of

British America; next to the United States (£235,323); next to the British West Indies (£178,551); next to other countries (£157,388); and the least to Britain (£21,736).

The returns for the whole province for the same year were—imports, £1,620,191; exports, £1,377,826. This, for a recently settled country, with a population of only 276,117 in 1850, betokens no small industry, enterprise, and progress. The following articles, exported mostly from other places than Halifax, are of interest:—Apples and plums (£6,244), butter (£24,704), coals (£85,682), gypsum (£17,479), lumber (£95,176), potatoes and vegetables (£77,315), fire-wood (£19,877).

With about 1,000 miles of coast, innumerable convenient harbours, and waters swarming with excellent fish, the Nova Scotia fisheries, already important, as will be seen by the above returns, are yet believed to be capable of vast extension. With such stores of wealth in the surrounding waters, valuable coal and iron and other mineral treasures, and its fortunate geographical position, Nova Scotia will one day occupy a high position in the commercial world.

On the opposite side of the harbour, at a distance of about a mile and a half, is the village of Dartmouth, which seems to be thriving, notwithstanding some serious checks it has received. In 1751, the year after it was founded, it was the scene of an attack by the Indians, who surprised it during the night, scalped several of the settlers, and carried off a number of prisoners. Some of the inhabitants of Halifax put off to their assistance, but the Indians had retired before aid could reach the unfortunate colonists. Thirty-four years later, a very promising whale-fishery trade was established at Dartmouth, which, if not interfered with, might have gone on and flourished, and proved of great value to the province. In 1787 seventeen vessels were fitted out, navigated by 238 men, the proceeds of which year's voyage, amounting to £27,500, were exported to London in the following year. But this growing trade was suddenly checked. The British Government, anxious to oppose the French, who were fostering a similar trade at Dunkirk, induced the Dartmouth seamen to establish themselves at Milford Haven, in England, and soon Dartmouth became almost a deserted village. A small steamer plies every half hour between Halifax and Dartmouth, the deck of which, as it was going backwards and forwards, I found a very agreeable promenade when I desired a little exercise, without wading through those sloughs of despond, the mud rows or melted snows of Halifax. The Dartmouth boat was quite an ethnological study. There were to be seen, within a space of a few square yards, specimens of three races, from far apart regions of the earth's surface, the Caucasian, the negro, and the Indian. And all ranks were to be met with there. The premier, leader of the government during the greater part of the time when I was in Nova Scotia, was frequently to be seen there; he resided in a pretty villa in the woods near Dartmouth. He was a man of a tall, striking figure, venerable aspect, and quite a "distinguished" appearance, who impressed you at once with the combined idea of gentleman and man of high intelligence. Mild and courteous in his manners, with thought, sagacity, dignity, and many cares written in his countenance, he might have been selected from among ten thousand as the type for a senator or judge. Of his appearance in court a local paper says most justly, "There is that about him which tells you he is the greatest there." " Why sits he there, while in the motley crowd that is around and above him [on the bench] there is not one equal, scarcely one second to him? The judge who listens to him knows and feels that he is fitter to be his disciple than his teacher, yet the bench has never received him, and perhaps never will." This is too true. Universally respected in the province for his estimable character and long and honourable career, he has yet been deprived of the reward so justly due to his great services by the unfortunate system prevalent in public appointments, which virtually, though not so directly as in the United States, vests the election of the judges in the people. In Nova Scotia one must "stoop to conquer," and stoop pretty low. This gentleman was above such artifices. But he commands the sympathy and esteem of the education, the intelligence, and the respectability of the province.

There, too, we may see the pride of the colonies, the brave and hardy settler, who has laboured night and day at digging, draining, fencing, and manuring, at felling trees and clearing away stones, who has conquered the wilderness and succeeded in turning the desert into a garden, and has enriched his country while he has made himself independent. He is lord of the soil, pays no rent to landlord, has a comfortable and tasteful wooden cottage, with a pretty garden around it, keeps his own little vehicle, and has probably been over at the markets at Halifax, where he has business once or twice a week, and where he has a snug balance at his banker's. He is clad in gray homespun, with an easy wide-awake hat, and most probably exhibits the steady, persevering Scot in his countenance and dialect—a true Anglo-Saxon in speech, features, and character. He looks a little rough at first, but this is only the effect of the out-door, somewhat rugged life he has led; and on conversing with him, you find him, like his hat, quite wide-awake, well informed, and intelligent, perhaps a little puritanical in his ideas.

On the deck of the same little vessel may be seen numbers of a far different race, anything but the pride of Nova Scotia, the unlucky negroes, who abound in Halifax and the vicinity. During the last war with the United States some of our ships captured a number of slaves, and took them to Halifax, to be free, to be frozen, and to starve. In them Nova Scotia truly caught a Tartar. They have a settlement a few miles from Dartmouth, where they cultivate a little land and carry on a few simple branches of industry, such as making brooms, casks, etc.; and they may often be met in the Dartmouth boat, bringing their produce to market, or returning with their little purchases.

With all their industry, they are in but a poor way, scarcely able to make the two ends meet. With their inferior organization and the universal prejudice against them (as strong in Nova Scotia as in the Northern United States), they cannot compete with the intelligent and energetic Caucasian, and mostly sink to the very bottom of the social scale. It seems a very hard case, that of the negro race in North America; they are not wanted, there seems no place for them. In the words of Mr. Seward, "the white man needs this continent to labour upon," and he takes it. In spite of their extreme and evident poverty, however, a happy disposition proves some compensation; they seemed a light-hearted and cheerful people, always laughing and making merry—

"Contented wi' little, and canty wi' mair."

It was strange to hear these dark-skinned Ethiopians speaking a far purer English than the majority of the emigrants from the old country; but it was still more startling when you came suddenly upon them, as on turning a corner, to have forced upon you instantaneously the resemblance to another order of the class mammalia; to which, however, according to some hypotheses, we may all be more nearly related than is agreeable to reflect upon. While such is the condition of the majority of the negroes in or near Halifax, it would be unjust to that unfortunate and ill-used people not to mention two cases in that city (and there may be more) of negroes, apparently of unmixed blood, who by their industry and intelligence had obtained a superior and very respectable position.

Yet another and a widely different tribe of men is to be met in the Dartmouth boat—the Red Indian, the heathen and barbarian, the original owner of the country, from which the Christian and civilized man is gradually exterminating him. The Nova Scotia Indians, the Mic-macs, are the gipsies of the country; and, indeed, the cast of countenance of some Indian lads I have seen in New Brunswick and Nova Scotia frequently recalled to my mind the faces of gipsy boys in Murillo's well-known pieces. In head, form of feature, expression and air, we say at once, here is a very superior race to the negro. Yet the latter surpasses him (speaking generally) in steady industry and other capacities for civilization, which are unsuited to the lord of the prairie and the forest. Although some tribes of Indians in Canada and the United States have acquired steady habits, and settled down to regular employments, this is not the case with the generality of the Micmacs. They live in their wretched wigwams in the woods, fish, hunt (where that can be done now), sometimes make brooms, cricket-bats, baskets, and beg. On passing a wigwam, the children run out and salute you with " Gie me coppa!" (give me coppers). Their attire is most dilapidated, and rather scanty, generally cast-off clothing supplied them by the settlers. The chiefs have sometimes a fine light blue coat, made expressly for themselves, ornamented with bead-work (and the females, now and then, have pretty head-dresses); but the generality are dressed in second-hand clothing, and have very much the look of reduced gentlemen; for, in spite of all, there is something like a gentleman in the aspect of the Indian. He speaks little, is grave and reserved; when you pass him on a country road he nods, but without a word, or the least indication of a smile. He appears like a ruin crumbling to pieces, and, like it, will soon pass away and be seen no more. Many of the females are handsome, fine-looking women, who, suitably dressed, and in other scenes, might be taken for brunettes of the Caucasian race. The Indians seem, generally, to live a most precarious, wretched existence, though the

Government is not unmindful of them, giving them blankets and a few other supplies during the winter.

The arrival of the Admiral's ship, or fleet, on the station, is an important event in Halifax. This usually takes place in May, the squadron spending the winter in the West Indies, the summer in Halifax. The vessels lie quite sheltered, and close to, or a stone's throw from, the shore, so that they are of easy access to the citizens, and officers and men can get ashore at all times, in a few minutes and with little trouble. Then commences a round of visits and entertainments. There is a large house appropriated to the Admiral, and he usually keeps open doors; the citizens invite the officers, and frequently the latter return the compliment, by giving a ball on board ship. All the flags are put in requisition, and formed into a gay canopy above the deck; the upper deck is the reception-room; the lower deck, where the Admiral's band is stationed, the ball-room. Boats are at the wharf to take the company out; they skim gaily over the blue waters with their precious cargoes, and set them safely and pleasantly on board, for it is never very rough in Halifax harbour. Promenading, introductions, chit-chat, admiring the scenery, etc., go on for a while; soon the ball, or bonnet-dance, begins; there is a "sound of revelry" on the deep : Nova Scotia's capital

* * * had gather'd then
Her beauty and her chivalry, and bright
The lamps shone o'er fair women and brave men.

The young officers are very happy, and make some of the young civilians a little miserable. Sometimes we see a lively captain, or one still higher in rank, who is not very young, enjoying the dance as much as his juniors, and monopolizing the fairest, for the elderly officers have an excellent taste. Those who do not dance, stand on the upper deck, and survey the lively scene below, or walk about, inhaling the fresh and exhilarating breeze; some dive down amongst the berths or the cabins, to visit friends and try the grog. Ere long, the jolly tars exhibit their hospitality, and take each his partner down-stairs to a sumptuous collation, where capons and cannons, roasts and ropes, blanc-mange and bullets, custards and cutlasses, wine, women, and war, mingle in odd contrast and confusion. This is the most agreeable entertainment given at Halifax; the sea, the sky, and the rest of the natural scenery around, the uniforms and the breezes, the flags and the bullets, and the thoughts of other scenes acted upon these decks, give it a piquancy that no ordinary ballroom can have. The army also returns the hospitalities of the citizens by one or two balls during the winter season. It is the army and navy that keep Halifax alive; but not for nothing. They capture a good many fair prizes, some richly laden. I should advise any young ladies in England, who have very particular friends in the army or navy, to keep a sharp look-out after them when they are ordered to Halifax. It is rather a dangerous locality; the merchants are rich, and their daughters are fair, and the mingled charms and dollars have a powerful effect upon her Majesty's service. There are delightful pic-nics in the summer season, for which the surrounding country is favourable; and these are often followed by an interesting Church service, beginning with " Dearly Beloved," and ending with " Amazement," at which a gallant officer and Halifax belle play leading parts. A good-looking young officer, who is known not to be dependent on his pay alone, and to be of a genteel or aristocratic family, is beset with kind attentions. There never was so popular an Admiral on the station as one who declared on arriving at Halifax that he intended to have his miserable bachelors made happy there, and set about making his words good by entertaining hospitably, at Admiralty House, and introducing the navy to the beauty and fashion of the place.

This little colony, with a population less than that of Manchester or Glasgow, and a revenue of about £125,000 sterling, has a cumbrous machinery for its government, like that of Great Britain. There is a *House of Assembly* of fifty-five members, elected by universal suffrage at least once every four years; a *Legislative Council* of twenty-one members, nominated for life by the Crown, that is, by the Colonial Government; a Governor; a Cabinet, called the *Executive Council;* and a national debt, incurred for the railway, to complete the resemblance. The leading officers of State, who, with sometimes one or two without office, form the Executive Council, are, the Attorney-General, the Solicitor-General, the Provincial Secretary, (Home Secretary), the Financial Secretary (Chancellor of the Exchequer), and Receiver-General (resembling the British Board of Treasury). The Chairman of the Railway Board is sometimes a member of the Executive Council. The members of the Legislative and Executive Councils are dignified by having prefixed to

u

their names "The Honourable," the one only title found amongst the republican institutions of North America. The session of Parliament usually opens about the end of January, and continues from two to three months. The members are paid 16s. sterling per day and travelling expenses; and it is said that some of them have no objection to see the session prolonged. They do not work very hard, meeting usually from three o'clock till about seven in the evening; but they talk very hard; a debate often continuing for a week or ten days—sometimes a fortnight or more.

The prime movers in the politics of Nova Scotia, when I was in the province, were the struggles of two lawyers for the succession to the chief justice-ship; the efforts of a demagogue whom "the people" delighted to honour, and his hangers-on to be provided for at the public expense; and the malignant and intolerant feeling towards Roman Catholics entertained by a section of the Presbyterian body. There was no want of gentlemen who had the real interests of the country at heart, but their voice was comparatively feeble and powerless; there were other and better motives in operation, but it was notorious that their force was trifling and really of no avail compared with that of the above three, which were at the bottom of political movements in this distracted little colony.

Acadie is no longer the home of the happy. It is, in two words, a political pandemonium, if there is one upon earth. The governor has described it most truly in the words quoted at the head of this chapter. The discords, coarse personalities, bitter strife, heartburnings, and riots with bloodshed, that take place in Nova Scotia are discreditable to a free and civilized community, where no class can complain of privation or any sort of political oppression. The people are well off, in fact, all thriving; they are very lightly taxed, enjoy the most perfect religious and political freedom, and have neither king, aristocracy, nor established church to set up for standing grievances. But they have demagogues who want places, fiery religious zealots who want power, and universal suffrage for these to delude and make a tool of. The grand struggle is for the loaves and fishes; and this aim is proclaimed with surprising candour, without any hypocritical disguise as a homage of vice to virtue. Shortly after I arrived in Nova Scotia, the premier openly gave his sanction to the American political maxim, that "To the victors belong the spoils." That was the first great political principle I heard

set forth in Nova Scotia. He knew well, no
man better, the odious character and injurious
tendency of such a line of action, and tried to
save himself by saying, "The principle that ' to
the victors belong the spoils' I will neither
affirm nor deny;" but as he did not deny it,
and practised it, people saw in these equivo-
cating words only another example of—

> "A hovering temporiser, that
> Canst with thine eyes at once see Good
> And Evil, inclining to them both."

This vicious policy of removing public officers
for a mere difference of political opinion was
first practised on a large scale by General Jackson, President of the United States, who is
said, within a month after his entrance into
office, to have removed more persons from the
public service than during the forty years previous since the adoption of the Constitution.
He had supporters in the Senate, where it was
boldly preached, in 1831, that "to the victors
belong the spoils of the vanquished." But the
American people protested against it as "detri-
mental to the interests, corrupting to the morals,
and dangerous to the liberties of the people."
It is, however, unavoidable in countries such as
the United States and Nova Scotia, where the

public men that lead the people are mostly trading politicians, whose means of existence depend on getting hold of the spoils of the vanquished. In the latter province lately, a new party attaining power dèprived a registrar of deeds of his office to find a place for a partisan.

It may be asked, Why is that class of public men so predominant? Where are the solid, intelligent, honest, independent gentlemen of the country, who ought to be the true leaders of the people and statesmen to rule in the councils of the nation? There are such in Nova Scotia; but they are few in number, because it is a small, poor country, where there is no landed aristocracy, not many wealthy merchants, and the great majority are labourers and small farmers and shopkeepers: and those few mostly stand aloof from politics, for the same sort of reason for which one gives a sweep or a coalheaver a wide berth in passing him. They shrink from contact with the rough blustering demagogues who are called into existence by the easy prey which they find in the simple-minded, impulsive, ill-informed, and readily deluded class that, by the wide extension of the suffrage, swamps every other.

If English legislators who advocate extension of the suffrage were to spend some time in the British American colonies, or in the United States, I do not think they would feel inclined to carry such extension far. They would have before them too many evidences that a wide constituency is not a discriminating constituency, and becomes an easy prey to the reckless demagogue or place-hunter. Representation in proportion to mere numbers, as in America, has undoubtedly proved a failure; it does not at present produce good government, and its prospects for the future are anything but encouraging. Again, and again, I have heard leading men on both sides of politics in Nova Scotia express their regret that universal suffrage had been established in the province, and their determination to make an endeavour to limit the franchise in some way, such as confining it to real freeholders. A step backwards is very difficult in such a case; they will probably find it so difficult that they will not dare to make the attempt. It seems to be generally supposed that there is a necessity for widening the doors of the suffrage in Britain; if so, the experience of America seems to show that it should be done very cautiously and gradually, according to classes, not mere numbers, and only in the direction of those who, by some unequivocal test, are known to be educated and intelligent. A property test would not only be inadequate, but offensive to large classes. Surely some educational test (or some test, which, if not ostensibly, is virtually an educational one) might be devised, which, by the extension of means of procuring instruction, would be accessible to numbers in every class of society, and which, while representing all classes and interests, would avoid overwhelming the constituency by one class, and that the least qualified for its temperate and judicious exercise.

While this unhappy little colony is thus afflicted by the place-hunting demagogue class, it is also distracted by religious feuds. A new sect, which was not wanted, intruded itself into the country, and has endeavoured to make itself appear of use and importance by insulting and offensive attacks on the Roman Catholics, who form a large proportion of the people. The bad feeling thus created was greatly increased by a series of letters attacking both Irishmen and Catholics, written by the Hon. Joseph Howe. This gentleman (at the time Chairman of the Railway Board) fell into a quarrel with some Irishmen, from alleged interference on their part with his efforts to recruit for the Crimean army in the United States. Irritated by this, and, it is said, desiring to overthrow the Government, with which he was connected, which was supported by the Roman Catholics, and to unite with the opposition, he commenced a Protestant and Saxon crusade against Catholic and Celt. The letters which he published on the subject, in the *Morning Chronicle*, first attracted my attention to Nova Scotian politics. They were calculated to rouse up the worst feelings between Catholics and Protestants, and, undoubtedly, had this effect. He was not contented with the questions of the day, but went back hundreds of years to show how bad Roman Catholics and Irishmen had been, as if he wished to undo the good work of the great conciliatory act of 1829, which every Government since, and every governor of a British colony, have so faithfully endeavoured to carry out. It is doubtful if a series of letters of so mischievous a tendency ever before emanated from a public man in the British dominions. But he quite outwitted himself. The opposition spurned his advances; the Catholic members in the House of Assembly abandoned the Government, joined the other party in a body, and a vote of want of confidence was carried, which sent Mr. Howe and the rest of his party into the cold shade of opposition for three years. Then came a bitter contest for power. Numbers, for years previously in close alliance with the Catholics, and who had not before been known to be anything in particular, found themselves, all of a sudden, zealous Protestants and fierce No-Popery men. An alliance with Catholics was now denounced as disgraceful, and a Protestant alliance sprung into activity; the most absurd and outrageous calumnies were circulated and believed by the good, simple, country people. A desperate agitation was carried on over the whole country; riots, in which one was killed, took place; the moderate, reasonable men had no chance in the struggle with the zealots and the rowdies; and when Parliament was dissolved, in 1859, the intolerant party carried the day, though by a small majority.

The coarse and insulting language employed by several of the public men, and the generality of the press, the offensive personalities, the angry recriminations, the misrepresenting and finding fault with everything that a political opponent says or does, indications of the rude contests of an inferior class for place, are sickening to a stranger and to the more respectable portion of the community. The bitter feelings thus roused spread to still lower classes, where they pass into brutality and violence; and it is no exaggeration to say that the style of the press and that of some of the leading men, have a powerful influence in corrupting and brutalizing the people throughout the length and breadth of the land. An English statesman (Tierney, I think) said pleasantly, "It is the business of the opposition to oppose everything, and turn out the Government." That, taken literally, and carried out as offensively as possible, faithfully represents the course of the opposition when I was in the province.

In the House of Assembly of Nova Scotia, members allow themselves extraordinary license in personalities. Amongst others, one very notable instance took place when I was in the province. A leading member—a man who is said to have had some education, and should have known better (whom we may call X)—having disputed the accuracy of some statement made by another, said, after relating the well-known story about Bruce the traveller, "Bruce after this was known by the name of the Abyssinian lyre. But here we are more fortunate; for we have one of native growth, known in every corner of the province as the Nova Scotian Lyre. Mark me, Mr. Speaker, the Nova Scotian L-y-r-e," spelling the word carefully, letter by letter. But in a very few minutes he must have repented heartily of this mean slander. His opponent, whom we shall call Mr. S.—in every respect a gentleman, as well as a man of talent—rose and administered to Mr. X. such a castigation, as hardly ever was given before in a Legislative Assembly. X.'s public career had been somewhat tortuous and tricky. S. had a retentive memory, and had it all before him. He described several of the leading incidents, with the turn necessary for his purpose, and at the end of each, turning to X., and looking him full in the face, he said, "And now, I am sure we must all agree with the hon. gentleman when he says that there is a L-y-r-e in Nova Scotia." He went over several awkward transactions in this manner, X. looking as if he wished to sink into the earth. Gentlemen present described this scene as one of the most extraordinary they ever witnessed in a public assembly. It would be well if such attacks as that made by X. were the worst; but some members (certainly few) will go further still; they will drag before the House something in the private lives of their opponents if they think by so doing they can damage them or wound their feelings. One member taunted another (a man as far his superior in intellect and every other respect as one man can be to another) with having negro blood in his veins.

Some slanderous tittle-tattle was going about as to a leading member—untrue, and, even if true, entirely of a private nature; his adversary threw it in his teeth in debate. He was instantly challenged to produce proof, denounced as a slanderer, called upon for his authority, defied to repeat it where not protected by his parliamentary privilege. He had nothing to say, but that he heard it when down in the country. It is doings such as these that deter many of the best qualified men in Nova Scotia from entering into public life. They naturally shrink from exposing themselves among persons who cannot differ with an adversary without hinting that he is a L-y-r-e.

A member who takes the lead in this style of attack once so far forgot himself as to read a lesson on the subject to another. This called forth a veteran, who remarked—" Sir, I listened to the hon. gentleman's remarks on the subject with a strange feeling. The past and the present mingled. Why, sir, the very foundation of his career was laid in slander and abuse, not alone by attacks on public men, but by assailing character in private life, by lacerating the tenderest feelings in the domestic circle, and forcing the shafts of calumny and detraction into the quiet of men's homes."

These offensive personalities of leading men have a very bad effect on the people.

The people of Nova Scotia seem to be endowed with much natural talent;* and although many of the best men avoid political life, from the roughness and violence which mingle with it, still a good deal of ability finds its way into the House of Assembly. There are one or two members of that House, sufficiently notable and noisy, of whom I prefer not to speak further than to say, that they are considered by many, on whose information and judgment I confide, as the bane of the province. Of others, it is a pleasure to speak. Two of these, the Hon. J. W. Johnston and Charles Tupper, Esq., would grace any Legislative Assembly. The latter, I feel confident, would rise to distinction in the British House of Commons. Without any oratorical pretensions, he has such command of appropriate language, is so clear and distinct in his statements, so animated and forcible in style, goes so directly to the point, never overlaying it, is altogether so business-like, and, at the same time, with a most capacious memory, is so ready and feli-

* Many of the youth of all classes in Halifax came under my notice, as apt, clever, intelligent, and with as fine dispositions as any class of boys I ever had experience of.

citous in reply, that he seems to have all the qualities for what Sir Robert Peel was described to be, a great member of Parliament. In the places where I lived, I had the pleasure of meeting several members of the Assembly, as independent, faithful, intelligent, and valuable public servants as any country can boast of. Among these were my much esteemed friends "The Doctor,"* and the late Financial Secretary; but, alas! they were against proscription of the Catholics, and against loading the country with debt to build railways that would barely pay the cost of working them (if so much), and were therefore relieved by their constituents from their parliamentary duties at the last election.

There is nothing more to be deplored in some of the British Colonies than the character of the appointments to important public offices. I saw and heard of many instances in different colonies, a few of which I will mention. In one colony, a lawyer, by the turn of the political wheel, came to be the leader of the Government; he had a brother, who had not been

* Of seventy-three members of the two Legislative Assemblies, four were medical men when I was first in the province; there were also numbers of lawyers.

fortunate in life, and, at the time, as a last resort, was keeping a small store; something must be done for him; this is too precious an opportunity to be lost;—he is appointed to organize and superintend the *education* of the country! In another colony, this important and delicate office was conferred on a man who had been notorious chiefly for his coarse and virulent attacks on the Roman Catholics (who formed a large proportion of the people whose education he was to superintend), and to whom he had rendered himself peculiarly offensive, and who was well known to be disqualified, as being rough and overbearing in his manners. But he was a follower of the party in power, had served them, and must have something given to him. There was no want of able and accomplished men fitted for the office, of character and standing, and courteous and gentlemanly bearing; there is abundance of ability in the colonies. A high judicial office was vacant; there were two gentlemen peculiarly fitted for the office, learned, eloquent, eminently skilled in the law, of the highest character, universally esteemed and respected, who would have done honour to the bench in any country. Every intelligent man in the province knew that the choice ought to fall on one of these two; the difficulty was to choose between them. But neither was taken; a party politician was appointed, the opposite of the above two gentlemen, in almost every particular, whose qualifications were a certain pompous school-boy power of declamation, and having truckled to an unscrupulous demagogue, who needed a legal tool, and whom he served by gaining an election by the force of a weighty purse. This was felt, by every man of education and respectability in the country, as a heavy blow and great discouragement to the public service. What high-minded man will look to that service as a means of honourable support, when preferment is to be reached only by means to which he cannot stoop, when the most eminent qualifications for a judicial office are passed by, and it is given to him whose gift is to hang by the skirts of those who sway the mob? Another case may be judged of by the following reply to the holder of a high office in the colonies, given by the editor of a newspaper, whom he had roughly assailed:—" He," the editor, " has never been placed in charge of an important public office, and therein embezzled large sums from the revenues of his country; he has never, when entrusted to disburse a large sum of money for a specified object, surreptitiously appropriated to his own use some hundreds of pounds of it, and retained them until accident led to a discovery of the fact." Similar statements have been openly made by other newspapers, and by respectable members of the House of Assembly.

The Governor of a British province is in a peculiar position; one not very enviable. He is cut off from society of his own class and standing, and from many of the intellectual enjoyments of civilization; and often society, by no means the best the colony affords, is thrust upon him by the state of parties. He is accustomed to the quiet, steady, orderly working of the British Government, and has to witness and sometimes sanction proceedings that his respect for law and courtesy revolt against. He is soon made to feel that he is viewed as a mere ornamental appendage, to be endured while the British connexion is maintained, and as long as he is subservient to the rule of the majority, but in case of differing from that majority, threats to appeal to the Home Government, and indications of a desire for the American system of electing governors, are pretty plainly conveyed to him. He may be thankful if, on failing to please all the strange

x

people he is called upon to meet, he escapes being subjected to such outrages as some of the discontented threatening to hire a nigger to horsewhip him. Lately, the leader of the opposition did appeal to the British Government against the Governor of Nova Scotia; but the latter was entirely supported by the Home Government, as well as by the moderation and intelligence of the province. In his letter to the Colonial Secretary, seeking redress, the Opposition leader had the singular good taste to hint that the Colonies might become Republics!

The press of Halifax carries out to extraordinary lengths the peculiar style indulged in by some of the public men of the country. I shall never forget my astonishment at the first newspaper I saw in that city—at the coarse Billingsgate with which it assailed the judges, gentlemen deservedly esteemed and honoured in the country. Without one or two specimens, it would not be believed that such a press could exist in the British dominions. An editor and leading politician is described as follows:—" The drivelling toady—the sour bigot —the impudent jackanapes, who dared to call some of his constituents perjurers, and to defame the noble kingdom from which most of them are sprung; —— who plotted with ——

to get up the Titus Oates' cry; —— the sneak, with vacant face and dark heart, has fallen." Then follows something so indecent that it cannot be quoted. The editor so complimented, thus, in his turn, characterizes a brother editor:—"The most universally despised and detested creature in the province;" and another paper says of one of the foremost men of the country, "If he is a great man, he is also a great blackguard." These are three out of hundreds that might be adduced; and, from a notable *religious* paper, that enjoys a bad pre-eminence, we might select specimens of such brutality (there is no other word for it) as would hardly be believed when seen. But the press of Halifax is a pluralist, of a kind that is not to be endured. Besides being wicked, it is intolerably stupid. A Halifax paper is the dearest article sold in the colony, though only a penny. It is small, less than the London *Globe*, and three pages are filled with advertisements. These are not to be despised when they are new, but a considerable proportion are old, kept up to save the trouble and expense of looking out and setting up new and interesting matter. I have seen often an advertisement of a meeting weeks after it had taken place. The one page reserved for news contains puffs of quack medicines, notices of extraordinary large cabbages, or a wonderful pig that weighs more than ever pig weighed in the world before; thanks for a piece of bridescake the editor has received, and his best wishes to the happy pair; or an intimation that some favoured restaurant has got a fine turtle or some delicious salmon; an acknowledgment of a bottle of hair-oil that has been sent; and long stories about every poor wretch that is found drunk and fined 5s. by the magistrate. Exhausted by these efforts, the editor fills up the remaining space by huge gaps between the paragraphs. While the world is teeming with events, the press with interesting and instructive works on history, biography, science, one finds nothing in the Halifax papers but party squabbles and abuse, and news such as the above. The debates in the legislative bodies are given about a fortnight or three weeks after they have taken place. You get in Nova Scotia the debate of any day in the British Parliament before the debate of the same day in the Nova Scotia Parliament appears. You learn American news from the British papers, European news from the United States' papers. The Boston papers speak of "the benighted press of Halifax." I once saw a Yankee in a Halifax hotel, with time hanging heavy on his hands, take up paper after paper, laying each down in about three minutes, and when he had perused them all, he exclaimed, with a sigh, "Ah! a Halifax paper don't last a man long." And these papers are the only literature that reaches a large portion of the people of Nova Scotia.

When on my way to Nova Scotia I was greatly disappointed and discouraged by the bitter contempt with which I heard Canadians and Americans speak of the province and its capital. I consoled myself by attributing this to national prejudice. But I understood it when I saw the press of Halifax, and learned the style and conduct of several of the public men. These (the press and the public men) are the representatives of a country amongst foreign nations.

Halifax is a city with great capabilities and a great future before it; it is already one of the richest cities for its size in North America; there is no want of able men, of education, intelligence, and refinement; but they must not remain, as Mr. Prentice says, "dainty amateurs without moral courage;" they must come forward boldly, and rescue the country from the hands of those who corrupt and debase it, and degrade it in the eyes of other nations.

In conclusion, I may say a few words as to what the Americans think of us. Amongst the better informed classes, there seems to be quite a kindly feeling towards the English; of this I saw innumerable examples. Other feelings exist, but chiefly among the Irish part of the population, or less educated classes; though now and then a stump orator says pretty strong things against us—for some party purpose. The Americans generally seem to consider the British a good, well-meaning sort of people, but stolid, prejudiced, old-fashioned, wedded to antique forms, oppressed by the aristocracy, and intolerably slow. I have more than once astonished some intelligent Americans, by enumerating what we have done in the way of improvement, from the amelioration of our criminal code, begun by Romilly and Peel, down to our great free-trade and educational movements. They admitted readily that this was immense progress, more, perhaps, than ever any nation in the world achieved in so short a time without a revolution. Often, on comparing notes, the American declaimed strongly as to the wretched condition of our peasantry, which seemed well known to him, and our cumbrous, tedious, and costly legal forms. Even the Nova Scotian boasts of the superior simplicity and expeditiousness of his modes of legal procedure. I do not know that I was ever so much at a loss for defence or explanation, as when a wide-awake Yankee, who had been in England, urged our rejection of the proposal to decimalize the currency, as a proof of our being rather stupid, difficult to move, and quite behind the age. Judging from the inferior condition and uncouth dialects of many of the emigrants, they set us down as a semi-barbarous people, without education; and condemn us severely for our neglect of the great labouring class, as evinced by the rude, imperfect education, and the low condition of the agricultural labourer. Of the latter I heard again and again; the contrast between the wealth of the landlord, and the extreme poverty of those who mainly create that wealth, was ever ready in the mouth of the American.

For the man who labours with his hands, America, at present, while her rich, unoccupied lands afford outlets, seems the country where he has the best prospect of securing comfort and independence. Further, a man has there much better chances of rising in the world, if he is capable of that; and if he is a schemer or inventor, America is undoubtedly the field for him. For other classes, Britain presents advantages in the superior character of its literature of every description, the steady, solid, reliable nature of the people, the prevalent respect for law and the powers that be, and the very high standing, morally and intellectually, of those who lead and rule—men whom one is not ashamed to be governed by. The temperate climate of Britain renders that country more agreeable to live in than the extremes of North America, while, as an older and more completely cultivated country, England appears a perfect garden compared with the rural districts of the United States, or British America. A visit to America exhibits to our view a great, prosperous, and rising country, and a singularly clever, active, and ingenious population, with numerous points of interest; but makes us value all the more, the temperate clime, lovely fields and meadows, quiet, sober ways, solid institutions, estimable public men, and rich literature of Old England.

THE END.

www.ingramcontent.com/pod-product-compliance
Lightning Source LLC
Chambersburg PA
CBHW030749230426
43667CB00007B/893